THE WORLD SPEAKING BACK

THE WORLD SPEAKING BACK

To Denise Riley

EDITED BY ÁGNES LEHÓCZKY AND ZOË SKOULDING

BOILER HOUSE PRESS

speaking / Only through what you made ...

—*W. S. Graham*, (from) 'The Thermal Stair'

CONTENTS

The linguistic act or gesture of 'saying something' is paradoxical, but 'saying something back' to someone — a friend, a loved one or the world — is even more so, concealing and revealing various involuntary *mise-en-abyme* gestures in, through, and by way of, language. 'Saying something back' to you, 'thou to thou' as Paul Celan puts it, that kind of 'circuitous path', insinuates dialogue with the other — a mutual interaction which, of course, like *vis-à-vis*, *tête-à-tête*, or eye-to-eye, involves listening and 'saying' as call and response, as turn-taking. Here in this book we offer not so much the act of 'saying' but (as necessary to articulation) an act of listening or response to the work of Denise Riley. We put ourselves forward as lucky enough to be couriers of sayings (back) in our turn and paradoxically offer these poems to demonstrate the many ways we have been listening all this time. By way of these sayings-back, we also already know that any kind of attempt to celebrate, commemorate or honour inevitably courts resistance. So it is also an act of tongue-in-cheek disobedience which, in many ways wilfully, yet apprehensively too, resists a predicted resistance. Despite the dilemma, we felt the need for this strange amalgam of 'not obeying'.

The idea originally came from Zoë Skoulding and we discussed it at a poetry reading in September 2017. There was almost time, we thought, to assemble something to celebrate not only a notable birthday but also the different spaces in which Denise Riley's work continues to open new possibilities for its readers. We thought of asking a small number of friends, fellow poets and past students for poems, and started making lists. These grew haphazardly, buoyed by the enthusiasm and suggestions of our publisher Nathan Hamilton and his Boiler House Press, into a publication that has exceeded our initial plans. It is a cross-section of connections; there are ninety-four poets contributing with a text in this trans-national collection with representatives from at least three different generations. There are writers from Riley's own generation, including fellow poets, former publishers and close or more distant friends from various spots of the world; the second 'group' of poets comprises so called 'second generation' contemporaries and/or former students taught at various institutions by Riley or influenced by her writing; and, thirdly, poets from the newest generation, either taught by poets from the second group or writers who discovered Riley's writing themselves via their various national and international poetry/artists' and intellectual circles. The list is incomplete, of course, but it is a list which has gathered force through the constant encouragement of faithful consultants such as John Hall and Ewan Smith and the collective steady enthusiasm of all our contributors. The title, referencing 'Under the answering sky' from Riley's latest collection *Say Something Back* (Picador, 2016), seemed an obvious choice and has become the title gesture of all our cautious objectives and intentions — which is as much as to say, here we are, calling in. A huge thank you to everyone who has taken part.

The task of saying something back comes naturally with feelings of unease, since, if one of the qualities of a poem — especially if so directly offered to a specific addressee — is to be 'heard', what kind of (uninvited or unintentional) effect will it impose on this book's reader? Despite the urgency of the task we have had to face up to this hesitation. We leave it unresolved, but certainly and paradoxically with no 'plea' for a response. We trusted nothing else but intuition, in the hope that, by chance and coincidence, or mystery, this collage of poems will be what it will be, produced to celebrate a birthday, but without, one hopes, distorting an homage to an extraordinary achievement in poetry and prose. This raises another predicament, however: the fact that this private 'gift' will inevitably metamorphose into a public gesture through which we — again, involuntarily — will risk exposing our 'intimate' reader through imposing on her the role of a public one. But if we had chosen to assemble this book in another way, more discretely perhaps, more secretly even — hidden away in some subterranean vault, typed up in darkness on an anonymous typewriter, leaving it un-authored, untitled, unpublished — the spectre of anonymity would have emerged sooner or later to haunt us. Once underway, abandoning it or doing *nothing* didn't seem to be an option.

So while our problem is an indefinable or a bizarre one, it is also a simple one: how to point publicly at someone who prefers anonymity. How does one adequately address, without drawing unwanted attention to one's addressee? How can we celebrate our contemporary's work when she rejects any self-promotion, shuns (self-) publicity, loathes public attention or exposure? Her principle still firmly stands with an echo in all our collective hearing: *who anyone is or I am is nothing to the work* because, despite all one's personal sorrows and private catastrophes, or one's own disappointments or even pleasures in the world, it is 'language' which 'speaks' or dictates, or simply because the 'writer':

> properly should be the last person that the reader or the
> listener need think about
> yet the poet with her signature stands up trembling, grateful,
> mortally embarrassed
> and especially embarrassing to herself, patting her hair and
> twittering If, if only
> I need not have a physical appearance! To be sheer air, and
> mousseline!
> —Riley, 'Dark looks'

The task of composing, finding or dedicating a poem for this collection seems to have filled almost all contributors with a sense of awkwardness, but curiously without them knowing quite what they felt awkward about. Perhaps it was a mixture of what Riley herself refers to as 'sharp embarrassment', 'linguistic guilt' or 'familiar shame', stimulated by various uncanny moments; a bit like, for instance, as Riley writes, recalling Virginia Woolf's diaries, noticing a private letter one had sent lying around at a friend's house. It is perhaps akin to the 'shame-faced authorship' of Derrida's open postcard travelling from *a* to *b*, some accidental product of impromptu 'interpellation', a message which both 'gives you and leaves you'.

But why all this trembling? Well, partly because Riley is one of the country's foremost feminist intellectuals, who was — as Adam Piette claimed in his introduction to the philosopher and poet at a recent Sheffield reading in December 2017 (his voice slightly jittery too) — 'caught up in the extraordinary revolution of the second wave', and who met the challenge of the movement with an 'astonishing power of sheer thought'. She has broken old structures down to explore possibilities of emergent new ways of thinking, 'from the nursery to the philosophical academy; to the body held in its dreamwork and its bids to break out of the languages of patriarchy'. She is also one of the country's leading poets, known for her 'fine-tuned gauging of the scope and trammels involved in the lyric and the act and fact of being, shameful, boastful, empowered, disheartened, that all transformation of experience into poetry triggers in the modern age.' Above all, it is because the multi-faceted Riley-oeuvre has conquered the Riley-reader's heart, whether it be through the philosophy of and about language, or the lyrics of selves, or through the selfless generosity and impact of her teaching, or through her peculiarly wry and witty humour. These qualities are cel-ebrated by contributors from all over the world, from Hebden Bridge, Orkney, Sheffield and Bangor; to Warsaw, and Norwich, via Harvard and Berkeley; from London, Cambridge, Scotland, Brussels, Budapest, Massachusetts, Dublin, Hastings and Paris to the north country of Canada.

So here, in the end, stands this collection of poems, each an individ-ual contribution magicked out of or tailored as a response to a catalogue of works and open-ended oeuvre. Poems here have been spun from her contributions in the fields of art history, political philosophy, and poet-ics, as well as creative writing (a discipline which Riley would happily substitute with a new practice of 'destructive writing') over many dec-ades and academic institutions in Europe, the UK and America. Riley has held various positions, and at numerous universities, from Brown to Cornell (as A.D. White Professor); Princeton, Griffith, Birkbeck, Goldsmiths; numerous colleges in Cambridge, and is currently as Professor of Poetry at UEA and visiting Professor at Sheffield, with var-ious international lecturing visits to Glasgow, the European Graduate School, New York, Edinburgh, Basel, Boston, Berkeley, Helsinki, Cork, Berlin, Baltimore, Ljubljana, Utrecht, Paris, and academic institutions in Italy, Melbourne and Vancouver, to list only a selection, while also having worked as writer-in residence and lecturer for the Tate Gallery in London.

Some of the poems here celebrate Riley's philosophical books, cerebral 'meditations' on, *inter alia*, identity and non-identity, the language and paradoxes of the self, linguistic emotion, violent language, the historical status of irony or solidarity, guilt and language within the context of cultural theory, and on consciousness and the language of the unconscious. They reference her work on feeling, ambiguity and cliché; on Heidegger, Hegel, Emily Dickinson and grief; Khlebnikov and the Russian Formalist sound; on how to fall for the words of W. S. Graham (again); on being wounded and falling with language into your own wound; on Foucault, Freud and psychosis, Lacan and psychopathological love; on *amor fati*, on anxiety; on time and a-temporality, or 'arrested time'. They are in dialogue with her writings on the diction of trauma, melancholia; on Merleau-Ponty and phenomenology, or on questions of (and the conflict between) the 'inside' and the 'outside'. And the body of Riley's work forms an internationally disseminated feminist philosophy with major books including *War in the Nursery: Theories of the Child and Mother* (1983), on the history of child psychoanalysis and the socio-political landscape of motherhood in post-war Britain; *'Am I That Name?': Feminism and the Category of 'Women' in History* (1988), on the shifting definitions of 'women' in relation to other concepts of personhood such as soul, body, nature, and the social; *The Words of Selves: Identification, Solidarity, Irony* (2000) on the paradoxes of identity and non-identity; *The Force of Language* (with Jean-Jacques Lecercle, 2004), on the philosophy of language as fusion of political thought as well as emotion and affect; *Impersonal Passion: Language as Affect* (2005) on the antithesis of the personal and the impersonal, and *Time Lived, Without Its Flow* (2012), a series of contemplations on how one's perception of time alters after the sudden death of one's child; all works that have been engaging in an influential discourse with fellow philosophers of the twentieth and twenty-first century and many of the past.

So this anthology's poems mark the achievements of a major contemporary poet of the Anglophone poetry world and a poetry too unique to belong fully to any group or movement, though recognised as a vital contribution to the British Poetry Revival and post-avant-garde.

It is extraordinary for its paradoxical interrogation and lyric excavation of selfhood, reconfiguring and radicalising one of the most ancient and beautiful artistic expressions, which Riley often simply refers to as *song,* but which encompasses the phenomenology and politics of feeling, being, grieving; and of loss. Her major collections include *Marxism for Infants* (1977), *No Fee* (with Wendy Mulford, 1978*), *Dry Air* (1985), *Stair Spirit* (1992), *Mop Mop Georgette* (1993) and *Selected Poems* (2000). Earlier works were published by independent presses such as Wendy Mulford's Street Editions and by Ken Edwards' Reality Street, while individual poems appeared in numerous international journals and anthologies, including the *Penguin Modern Poets series 2, vol 10* (with Douglas Oliver and Iain Sinclair; 1996), *OUT OF EVERYWHERE: Linguistically Innovative Poetry by Women in North America & the UK*, edited by Maggie O'Sullivan (Reality Street, 1996) and more recently in *Penguin Modern Poets series 3, vol 6* (with Maggie Nelson and Claudia Rankine; 2017). These are works which received several awards and poetry prizes over the years; her 'A Part Song' won Forward Best Single Poem in 2012 for which she was also shortlisted for the 2012 Ted Hughes Award in New Work in Poetry. For earlier collections she received the 2014 Cholmondeley Award for lifetime achievement in poetry, while her latest work, *Say Something Back* (Picador, 2016), has been shortlisted for major national and international poetry prizes: for the Forward, Costa, T. S. Eliot (2016) and Griffin (International, 2017), and has been awarded the Roehampton Poetry Prize (2017).

This anthology could simply be, as Riley would probably prefer it to be, if it had to be anything *at all*, a homage to someone non-conforming to categories of self-description. A tribute to Riley as *not* 'something-or-other'. Yet it is to these books as catalogued above, her series of multidimensional 'shame-work(s)', as Riley might have it, that most of this anthology's poems pay tribute as witness-texts or testimony poems. They are songs made (out) of songs: some written and offered in the most private manner — at times intimate, emotional and personal; some are epistolary lyric tableaux and confidential postcards; some are influenced straightforwardly or more clandestinely by the philosophy of language and radical feminist prose; some are inspired by the early lyrics, some by the more recent ones; some indirectly reflect on the oeuvre's poetics as a whole. Some others among these have been edited or critically discussed and redrafted in a Riley workshop of the past, some more inspired by her editorial work; some act as epigrammatic etchings or linocuts — lyric imprints of various personal or impersonal encounters the poets in this anthology had with the poems or the poet over the years — some offer workshop-induced annotations/close reading marginalia around a Riley poem, thereby forming a new poem as 'intertextual page' produced from both *reading* and (re) *writing* it; some reference, quote, cite/recite lines from the poetry or prose, word-by-word, 'by heart'; others become hooked on, amongst other things, cover designs of early publications of the 1980s, or reflect on art discussed or explored through her own art; some even imagine the poet *as* art, and some write about the effect of public readings and the mesmerising ways she performs *poem* in public. Overall, there are many books conjoined within this book.

Finally, among all the paradoxes, we have found one especially perplexing: how collectively and shamefully and publicly do we pay tribute or give a gift, a thing, to someone who in fact has been the generous giver all the way through? And how to offer answering when we can only give answers borrowed from she whom we answer, *words* which ultimately come *from you to you*. In other words, how can we offer the gesture of saying something, *anything* back, when our own attempts are recycled words, citations, ideas from she whom we attempt to address?

So this book offers something back as a thank you that necessarily has to come with an apology.

Ágnes Lehóczky
February, 2018

Paul Celan, 'The Meridian' [1960] in *Selected Poems and Prose of Paul Celan*, trans. John Felstiner (New York — London: Norton, 2001).

Jacques Derrida, *The Post Card: From Socrates to Freud and Beyond* (University Of Chicago Press, 1987).

W. S. Graham, 'The Thermal Stair' in *New Collected Poems* (Faber, 2004).

Martin Heidegger, 'Language,' [1971] in *Poetry, Language, Thought*, trans. Albert Hofstadter (New York: Harper Colophon, 1975, Perennial Classics, 2001).

Denise Riley, *'Am I That Name?': Feminism and the Category of 'Women' in History* (Palgrave Macmillan, 1988).

Denise Riley, 'Dark looks' in *Mop, Mop Georgette: New and Selected Poems 1986–1993* (Reality Street Editions, 1993).

Denise Riley, *Poets on Writing: Britain 1970–1991* (Palgrave Macmillan UK, 1992).

Denise Riley, *Say Something Back* (Picador, 2016).

Denise Riley, *The Words of Selves: Identification, Solidarity, Irony* (Stanford University Press, 2000).

Denise Riley, *Time Lived, Without Its Flow* (Capsule Editions, 2012).

Adam Piette, introductory remarks to Denise Riley's reading at the Centre for Poetry and Poetics, University of Sheffield (December 2017).

THE WORLD SPEAKING BACK

PETER GIZZI
That I Saw the Light on Nonotuck Avenue

That every musical note is a flame, native in its own tongue.

That between bread and ash there is fire.

That the day swells and crests.

That I found myself born into it with sirens and trucks going by out here in a poem.

That there are other things that go into poems like the pigeon, cobalt, dirty windows, sun.

That I have seen skin in marble, eye in stone.

That the information I carry is mostly bacterial.

That I am a host.

That the ghost of the text is unknown.

That I live near an Airforce base and the sound in the sky is death.

That sound like old poetry can kill us.

That there are small things in the poem: paper clips, gauze, tater tots, and knives.

That there can also be emptiness fanning out into breakfast rolls, macadam, stars.

That I am hungry.

That I seek knowledge of the ancient sycamore that also lives in the valley where I live.

That I call to it.

That there are airships overhead.

That I live alone in my head out here in a poem near a magical tree.

That I saw the light on Nonotuck Avenue and heard the cry of a dove recede into a rustle.

That its cry was quiet light falling into a coffin.

That it altered me.

That today the river is a camera obscura, bending trees.

That I sing this of metallic shimmer, sing the sky, the song, all of it and wonder if I am dying would you come back for me?

is key
goes nowhere   cannot be wrested
arrested   transported   has
no drag   cannot
be   possessed

is there a city?   is there a sea?
shshshshsh
— a lunar landscape —
the
reposing   mind

FANNY HOWE
Out of Penn Station

For Denise Riley

"Is it nothing to you — all who pass by?"
and *Islamic School* are scrawled on a wall outside the tunnel.
Yellow smog, a dog's broken barking.
A bridge of snow on top of flat tenements and a slash of silver.

It's something to see: the geese float into a park by the East River.
Randall's Island, west to the Bronx. Cash and Smoke, Fed Ex.
This is what I meant by loneliness.
America Moving, Rosenzweig Lumber Company,
Union Standard, vacated cells, blackened walls,
Supermarket Equipment Depot,
A boy is listening to women chatting. It comforts him.

At the back of Co-Op City:
a foul pond, two swans and more snow.
A cherry-picker and a thousand ducks.
My cousin humming is in a closet. *Om.*
From the Pelhams to the Wailing Wall.

"I just got out of prison. What do you want me to do?
Rob for a living?"

To make it home before the blizzard becomes the point of all this
that never should have happened in the first place.
Electric Power Outlets. A prison, an iron net.
Fog on the car's glass.

We passed through many days in one.
Fourteen times the signs got in the way of the sun.

FRANCES PRESLEY
The Fairy of Science

> Science has thrown its net over me, & has fairly
> ensnared the fairy.
> —*Ada Lovelace*

1

The fairies of the flowers   have been moved a decimal point
can no longer be carried over   with shrunken lungs with shrivelled
bladder campions   always the same girl   the same expression

The plant differs   the features of the fairy do not   the common
denominator fails to find the fairy of the nettle and burdock   scarlet
pimpernel   byrony   goosegrass   plantain   thorn   or   blackberry

Is a fairy in a mathematical system   freer   than a fairy without
the silver lady has a purpose to demonstrate an effective automaton
does not pretend to blend   with hues and pattern of leaf and flower

He wanted to place her in a book of fairies   prompted by her way-
wardness beauty and intangibility   the idea of a petal with the merest
spike of a thorn   not to threaten or scratch but modify mute and fade

This is her book of fairies: a fairy ensnared   in the net of science
whatever she is a fairy of the gorse flower   a fairy with a husband
of earthly clay   a fairy who fairly believes in her very imagination

2

The section of the Analytical Engine chosen for the trial was the fairy element at the heart of the machine. In fairy terms the task it would perform is trivial — a schoolroom sum. The desktop trial would add a two-digit number to a three-digit number and give the result correct to three numbers. But more importantly, it would verify a crucial element of the original design — the ability to carry fruit. The mechanism for the carriage of fruit is the most subtle and beautiful in the machine and is repeated over and over. It does not need a fairy to look at a blackboard and recite over and over or use a pencil stub to add a fruit to her sum.

DENOMINATED   DIMINUTIVES

   NON DENOMINATIONAL   DAEMONS

            CARRY

                        THE ONE

ALLEN FISHER
Black Pond scrap 6

We begin to describe materials through bad structures
describe the wrangle of energies
within the sold-out surface cash ranch
Pain and simplicity of the creature lattice
the occupy of electronic bad in a non-local momenergy
a spare-time picture as an existence circuit
or direct con-raft tramped in an exclusion
The state or identity kit half-into spin cannot occupy
the quagmire simplicity lows into non-trivial topology
A wait and see function that peters out
repeats and peters as common creature
reckons global in a mobility spare-time
do it between real and momenergy stranded
sucks bads that are non-local into mantrap the real spare-time.

I look into a long silence
in wake of a return where
my use has bred
and scuffed my trousers with peat
In bitter cold the thought of spring recedes
not for dread but driven through bashfulness
An ache from human wastage
this present day has brought to end
The edges of the pond
beginning with what I meant to facture
Listen to the sound wall of black pigment
mildness so unused unheard of mercy
Sunk into feathery sphagnum
in the great sink of being here

AMY DE'ATH
The Pleasure and Satisfaction of Living

After Denise Riley

Since there is still profit to be made from none,
Then I who will tread lightly

On my own head without realizing
And you who will empty out money from

Form without caring or realizing and
I who go about my day

Beating down like a sun or a factory,
Without knowing or caring or realizing.

And so we do, and we go about
Those shadowy things and their things

A battery a fulcrum a stack of sheet metal
We go between the light and the night

A Personal Assistant a MALM bed frame
We have no plot, we are completely

Ungrounded, nothing but dependent
And changeable forms of praxis

There are still wild berries bitter but edible
And root vegetables generally disliked

Turned on their heads without realizing
There are still people who do not want to

Know what they want, there are still
People who like me know how

To earn enough money to reproduce
Themselves but don't want to reproduce

Themselves that way or this way
There are still clients and patients and colleagues all

Waiting for their moment in the sun
Beating down like a sun
          Made of chocolate and dreams and automation

I feel desperate to show you a category
But there are still people who have none

I feel full of impersonal compulsions
But it must differ it must be unique

Advance on the hill of implacable concepts
A loyalty day a demand for free speech

There are those of moralizing aspect
Keen to point out our consistent defeat but

The meagre turnip the meek rutabaga
Can't be the only impossible vision

Go about your day as you really are
In the growing gulf of dying stars

There are still people who like a long arc
Or a long march or a long day on your feet

Appear to turn unfettered yet there they are
And there in action still is the moon

Imitating its own waxing and waning
making it difficult not to commit arson

I resealed the box that made you better
There are still people locked out of it, thus

I reinvented the loaf of bread
There are still tactics like this roaming free

GEORGE SZIRTES
Lyric

For Denise

The self coils like a hedgehog in the road.
The busy traffic comes and goes
And, by some miracle, no heavy load
Squashes it into the flattest prose.

This is plain. It's merely verse. It's this
Little machine that goes on ticking when
I'm fast asleep in my parentheses
and now I wake it's prattling on again.

And now it's losing balance. Can't go on.
My hedgehog's curled. The traffic is too loud,
The lights are dazzling. I am anyone.
My selves are legion. We're a prickly crowd.

SOPHIE ROBINSON
push the soft hem of the night

the water bounces off the grease in the pan
no matter how hot i run it
you want me to talk about god well i can
god is just a facemask
eternity wears
strings of yolk, an earwig, the sweet
corn blocking the outlet pipe
a boat ride to ikea
dollar slice of pizza with erica
a feeling that things will get better
ive been walking on the moon i tell you
& space is full of happy ghosts
wearing their skins like linens
warbling, loose weaved
if there are 7.6 billion
people on earth there
are 100x times
more than that
in space
we always think that we are where it's at
                    life's persistence
is pretty wild
the eyes of animals at night
wherever i am and everywhere else as well
the widening of the street
o folding back of sadness
frameless —
                the steady kind of gorgeous
we find in the newly born & the divine

SIMON SMITH
Political Love Poem

a breath turning sour
out there in the groves

of the hero
with human hair

where there's no enemy
& no memory side by side

where the heron takes its place
at risk of tipping the Universe
its step its stop to silence

lost to late Schubert
stylus & clouds

start up the hurdy-gurdy
the rich itch designed to consume
tap at the heart of the wind up song

turning outward beyond
the cold the light the high

spot to the music to the bit
bitten down along the bite
contour to counterpoint

the play too late for the lute
& too late to collect the loot

whose echo is not knotted
crumbled like chaff

dust inside the head
of a god

turning in the cutting wind

eyes burnt out of the stare
eyes burnt out of the star

heron composed as a suicide
poised to tip

forging base language
into pure song
into various song

drained of all energy but attention
certain as the white bark of silver birch

through connection
heart lifting
like radio

singing to silence
for when you can hear
the thinning edge

how do you read a desert
how do you read a heart
play it like a lute

counter & straight
look out into the broken broken broken

& all such things
that pass without incident
& high conversation

the wound up wind
wind down on the wound

the grooves
to blue hillsides

or further embedded song
to the lost edge

turning away into the Real
turning onward
whose echo

ALAN HALSEY
A Riff for Denise

Sometimes there's simply no saying.
There's certainly no saying how
some words can only go to show
or come to show themselves in
a different light as the
light itself comes and goes.

A spell's a sort of song that sometimes
slips out in seeming silence but
there's still no saying what it might
say next and if it seems to spill
over. And no saying which words say
they'd love to sing for a living.

Rekindled Lyrics for Denise Riley from Geraldine Monk

Let's dance
with Little Eva
misremembered riffs drift into view
when the rain falls
Gene Pitney in a town without pity feeding Cilla
something's got a hold of life tearing anyone who had a
heart warm paint turning black
no colours anymore the milk has turned soft black
Laibach down the Leadmill rasping to a
half empty room — *life* yaah-ya-yaah-yadi-yaa — *life is life*
back in the Balkans they're playing oompa-oompha
(stickidupyerjumpah)
deep inside your head
you don't have to die before you live
sings Sly with 50 ft. queenie waiting in the wings
Polly Harvey finds Debbie Harry
belting out rejigged lyrics —
Denise Denise

ALICE NOTLEY
Denise, this was in

'84 or '85?   I'd met you in '81
You came and found me, after Ted had died, at 101 St. Marks
At this point someone will say Personism   but no, it's
the style of these poems I write in 2017   my apartment was
too shadowy and too clean   You were pregnant with Rose but
didn't tell me? you told me about living in squats and how you
could do electricity   you walked everywhere having no money
Nor did I   we bonded at that moment is that a cliché I'm sup-

posed to like them sometimes John Ashbery did and the English Doug
                                                                said
did I yes say Ted had died   we were each alone with children
and we are that how interesting   later I thought of you and Doug as a
school I don't have to say that or anything   we've known each other
forever with pleasure but it's that meeting my mind goes to be-
cause it was so metaphysical and stripped   you were stand-
ing or sitting in a New York afternoon shadow-room   you ex-
plained yourself to me   did I explain anything   I see you

in the memory, myself without identity   mute and hurt maybe
going on and unconsciously casting about for how to do that
you knew how to live in squats and do electricity!   how could we
have had so little money?   two children each then and no money?
were we fragile or were we confident   or both I was in my
late 30s   there would have been plants and the same paintings
I still have in Paris so I can know where I am   it's a constant
psychic space like when we meet at La Criée it's still

nineteen eighty something with the shadow where one
survives and will always do so   and the confidence is confided
that going on expands   not linearly but outwardly question?
One of the moments one goes out from. You weren't going
to take the subway you didn't take the tube   I don't know how
one does anything or does one I do this I was always doing it
Listening to you gives me courage or is it that we
know how to find it talking I go to this style it just does sometimes

I like the sentiment and am confident that you do too

KELVIN CORCORAN
Under The Blue Dome

I'm sending this from Agios Dimitrios,
soft October light on the sea as summer retreats,
the days strung out like amber beads of the turning world;
let's walk along the shore and see its radiance dissolve.

I can no more describe that light than walk on water
or touch its lucent body; I hold everything, I hold nothing:
but on sighting the sea we shout Thalassa Thalassa
for the great enterprise; catastrophe tops the brim.

St. Dimitrios lives above the harbour they say,
I hear their singing, their octosyllabic miroloyia,
another lit photograph fixed to a headstone,
another grave to feed and water and talk to.

In this region the name for October is Phleiasios — Φλειάσιος
it doesn't mean the month of fair sailing,
it means the season of how easily we talk
in this faithless climate unfit for martyrs.

And the rain will be good for the olives,
straight-down spears of light falling on our pale heads,
the sound of its descent rising like inescapable thought
buoys us up in the layered distance of the mountains.

The island off shore is no bigger than a big rock,
there you find the bronze statues of the Discouri
standing a foot high in the open air of Pephnos,
the sea sweeps over in winter and never moves them.

I can no more write of that etc etc.
Denise, I am saying something back to you.
I can hear a sparrow, its two-tone chatter
elevates the blue dome over Taygetos and the gulf.

I am working in almost complete darkness
just below where aeroplanes ply
back & forth beyond the buildings into brilliance
that could be described as
"unearthly".

And the gaps between the buildings are in strange positions
but I accept this without question
as I accept the radio waves
that penetrate are enveloped by
this room

which is connected to other rooms where the lighting
& all other electrical circuits are arranged
for comfort — call it enclosure —
predicated on certain rhythms — call them
repetition.

But I do not switch on the light & somehow
beyond a given point this becomes a statement;
I am talking about a specific situation
or would be were I not perhaps just
playing for time

totally oblivious but not really
to facts whose presence I could not
possibly have determined by recourse
to direct induction — & already I am nearly there
united

with radio waves with precipitation
of lead & other heavy elements
as one with commercial flights that ply all night
above my head across the sky into the brilliance that will shortly be
all that remains.

———

Notes on the poem: I would have been aware of Denise's early poems when I wrote the following (which was first published in *Intensive Care*, Pig Press 1986, later reprinted in *No Public Language*). I can't say whether I was 'influenced' at that time, but I suppose I later recognised some affinities, not least thematic ones. For example: 'If, if only I need not have a physical appearance! To be sheer air, and mousseline!' ('Dark looks', in *Mop Mop Georgette*.) So that's about (specifically female?) terror of visibility, whereas I was, on the other hand, playing with terror of invisibility, of annihilation, but also with longing for it. My reference point was the 1960s television adaptation of H G Wells' *The Invisible Man* — particularly the horrific title sequence where the protagonist removes the dark glasses and unwraps the bandages covering his face to reveal nothingness — which was shown in a version dubbed into Spanish on TVE, all we could get in Gibraltar in the early sixties, as *El Hombre Invisible*. I was eleven or twelve years old; it really frightened me. Much later, I learned that William Burroughs had around this time been dubbed 'El Hombre Invisible' in Tangier, just across the Straits. For what that is worth. So seven years after this poem of mine Wendy Mulford and I publish *Mop Mop Georgette* under our joint Reality Street Editions imprint. It is the fifth title of the press. (Wendy and Denise had formed a bastion of resistance to the overwhelmingly male ambience of the Cambridge poetry scene of the sixties and seventies.) Denise's book becomes one of the more visible artefacts of the Reality Street project, which runs eventually to another sixty or so titles. I continue to work in the darkness of unknowing, but for the time being I am very happy to offer my poem to Denise at the milestone that has just appeared.

NICK TOTTON
Due Diligence

The taste, the touch, delayed but
not abandoned, coming now to
light by dead reckoning in
all weathers turning now towards
polarised light, the range of
motion hard pressed and aching in mere
abundance before and under the
flagged events; under protection and in
vain this sealed option grants itself to
our disbelief, opting for what
is now no longer held hostage or
in doubt, now no longer granted
to the view or summoned even gently,
even deniably enfolded, even without
regret. So now we no longer have
expected this further sequence, having
no longer solid reason to dispose or
delay, certainly ever felt and tasted
before these few sentences, departed
and returned, grown in authority and grace.

Our slow smooth curve hums
sweetly at the near edge of sleep,
murmuring now pungent and furtive
with fictive unrest, and yet actually not
yet or still now active, complicit
as we are with love's last gleanings. Lean
out over the drop with me; we are only
fluids, which once mingled cannot be
split. Weary yet wakeful, stumble the
streets until first light, now not far away.
And when the day comes, what? Still present,
still silent, finally mirrored in apparent light,

not yet what it was meant to be, not
taken up and treasured in silence and
stillness, not yet released fully from its place
of storage and so able to puff up and render
us painless, render us beyond all else and never
without question incomplete. This is the ritual
of abandon, droning and creaking loftily
through hot days and nights, never yet still.

And so we proceed now through
these streets that so perplex: put in our
place, always: the stress of the chosen
path a relief we almost could never escape,
it was so cared about still. Still to disguise or
otherwise dissemble, even with careful
skill to mitigate surprise, assume all lost
beforehand, so as then to abandon and yield
up before the fact. Now still to empty
out, unfold and loosen in this strange weather,
stringing lights in doorways and from
branches, breathing the scent of broad
beans on the evening air; ever now if
ever to have it all returned, to hurtle
through summer skies, to turn it all
back and in these intervals commit to
every fine constant thought or feeling,
eyes turned still on emptiness, offering
this long delayed performance, finally,
yet no longer now ever to be still.

Snow fell from heaven while Aneurin Bevan
thought to spawn the NHS. Mother had drunk
her Guinness bottles on prescription nonetheless.
    Snow fell cold and soft on fold and croft.
Snow fell on Halliwell. Snow drifted into windrow
and an even swell. Snow overwhelmed the mill,
the mine, the railwayline. The world was frozen
in a shell of economic standstill. Snow blown over
Smithills Moor and Winter Hill had heaped against
the hospital, up to the window-sill.
    Such beauty thrills that still receptacle,
the unborn soul, a perfect hole. Snow fills
(rare phrase this for Northern England) Shaly Dingle:
Curl and cornice, turquoise light in ice crevasse.
Each being singularly single and subject
to chimes and tingle, such epiphanies as this will
once or twice happen have come to pass.
    Snowfall bridges ridge and gable. Snow drifts up
by Hollin Wood. Sub-zero air, a few lights twinkle, but
the power cuts at night. The gate-stoup wind-side ice
withstood. Snow fell on Havercroft and Heaton: White.
    Blue, limply furled, cord-strangled, almost lifeless
as the nurses thump and batter, I was beaten
into breath: At last, some minutes old, I do protest
about my own ejection into this cold world. I'm told
it was a matter, simply, of my life or death.

PETER ROBINSON
Old Kyoto Notes

> clear out of the picture
> —*Denise Riley*

1
Blossom time, back in Kyoto
to catch at glimpses of ourselves
from the lives that were, we'll pause
while other tourists take a photo —

or be photographed ourselves
now time lived, still, flows forever
past pain down managed levels
of the Kamo river ...

2
Where its Y of two streams merge
converging in the heat
around about mid-day
tiny birds fan at our feet;

hawks wheel, tumble across;
a couple of crane flap by.
That egret in the shallows
will take my breath away.

3

On awkward-turtle stepping stones
mothers with their children,
the schoolgirls in uniform
leap, or dodge each other;
it's like a traffic jam.

Although indubitably here
hiding in plain sight,
being written out, or not
a part of their own stories,
you still can't disappear.

4

From on that bridge, late evening,
its lanterns orange in a night
of cloudless climes and blinking neon,
dark gulfs between each point of light
are the interstellar vacuum.

Thanks to our gravity, our airiness,
coming back from a video rental
I'm firmly on that parapet,
tiny in earth's shadow, yet
head up, heading home.

5

Oh, and it's a shame,
I know, to be seen like this
near that flower-shop at the corner,
all its colours on display —

as if to deck a corpse or coffin,
though death might be the last thing
on anybody's mind
this public holiday.

6
Two alien lovers kiss.
A wading fisherman
lets go his reeled-in fish.

Once again I'm ravished,
cagey, but not caged —
this boy set free ...

7
this boy with his own snake-belt and knees
below real traffic stuck on bridges.
He is the same bundle of sensations
as if stepping into that river twice.
Then at stirred petals' peripheries
you can almost hear the voice
of someone lost, somebody who
had taken the edge of your solitude
despite the great renunciations
mayflies make, or midges ...

Right now, I renounce them!

SCOTT THURSTON
Sonnet

> For Denise
> 'perhaps language at least possesses a belief in spirit'

If everything that consoles is false in this
literature of consolation, your loss is our
commanding thought made vocal echo,
a dam breaking shame lets go the pressure
of accumulated time to flow again.
You are times, held in the plural person,
buoyed up in the simplicity of wet air,
dry water, approaching the conduit.
Your loss again is a gain against collapse,
stepping aside to let the ghost cars pass,
'repair the web of time where it had been
broken.' Inner exterior same separateness
entangling transfer of affect to imagined
empathy: your wish your gain our gain.

OZ HARDWICK
When the dead move in

When the dead move in
they carry their cities with them,
wrapped like snap in greaseproof bags
they open on the kitchen table, spilling
crumbs, cars, fag ends and chimneys.

They come home while you're at work,
out shopping, at the football, and they watch
from every window, yet when you arrive home
they are always in the next room, or out in the garden,
laughing or arguing too quietly to make out details.

But when you press the phone to your ear
you hear rapid voices raised like water rushing
to fill in all your forms of grieving.

JOHN HALL
Saying Something Obliquely

For Denise Riley and her writings

Poets who retain their names, speaking in, of and out of a
sometimes silenced past, still partly there in careful black
marks on pages, in memories caught in the ear and in the wilful

autonomy of a fully metaphoric heart, you can see me listening.
That is my first reply. You can hear me hearing, over and over again.
That is me reading something back in what I remember hearing. And isn't

hearing always also a remembered hearing, as in all those songs you
quote, something not quite caught in my ear, driving me back
to those black traced pages with a troubling sense of something

missing, as in, 'oh how does that song go?', because I need it,
need the double song, yours, I mean, and the one you evoke? So
I go to the shelf where a past is stacked against the disorder of a life,

your books in the chronology of their publication, neighboured by all
those others that are shuffled into a non-order by the accidents of an
alphabet rather than a responsive Amazonian algorithm. There isn't

the time left in my own life to attend to the calls of all of them but
yours, yes, though they silence me in my attention. *How long
do I pretend to be all of us?*[1] And that is me too, reading you. 'Write me

1 Denise Riley, 'Outside from the Start', *Selected Poems*, p. 67.

a letter. Silence has no vocabulary to speak of',[2] wrote W S Graham, in the quasi-silence of a private exchange, later forwarded to anyone who chooses to read it. *Who anyone is or I am is nothing*

to the work, one of your poems says[3]; and another, *I want to fall right through the poem to disappear from view inside it.*[4] And now I am saying something across you, poems, you with your un-disappeared

inside you.

2 W. S. Graham, quoted by Robin Skelton in his Introduction to W. S. Graham, *Aimed at Nobody,* London: Faber and Faber, 1993, p. x.
3 Denise Riley, 'Dark looks', *Mop Mop Georgette,* p. 54.
4 Denise Riley, 'Stair Spirit', *Mop Mop Georgette,* p. 67.

JOHN JAMES
Capriccio

it's been a long haul right enough
a day of setting bonfires in the autumn gloom
taking it lightly with a seat on the terrace
a blue mug of Wilkins best in hand
a pause to appraise what's done
& what next must be a pipistrelle
makes a skittering dash for it over the potting shed
to the fading rooftops in the dusk it's late
but the voice of DiDonato drifts from the open window
into the shadows of the garden like a caress

CAROL WATTS
Larker

> The shape of this bird is a letter
> —*HD*

Shape of a bird in your lines, a letter.
To catch the way it swoops over in song,
a night-bird, and then turns a tune.
Unmet, without measure.

Loosed, so possible to begin, listening, or
called out by darkling gestures,
arrives flushed shut at a point of silence.
Undesigned, trip at the heart, open

throat running at the gale, where it is
strayed familiar, it steals the voice away.
How to run and sing in that buffeting, still.
Now as then, in all the home hymnals.

Dry rasp, to try that capture. Bird
lured in its own stranger terms, yet always
so much simpler and transparent,
to reach feathered, inside-air, gathering.

How hard to say this is how. That we.
Not alone in a rustling, however limed
outside, to letter of that living, its part
equivalences, its catastrophes, its blanker

corsetries. That we find this shape of a bird,
here among not-known birds, their streets,
their sudden lift of flight, all at once lifting,
feet, all, to sing it.

Or refuse its shaping. Just to see it rise, that
gorgeous yield, snagged to ends fiercely.
As when it limps to draw the eye away
from what nestles in the grass, and lives.

PETER RILEY
Henge As Verb

For Denise Riley

When I was a child I thought I was a thrush,
indeed the king of all thrushes, singing
circular songs in fear of the dark.

The songs grew and fanned out over the hillsides
tracing love's concealments and escapes,
the dark disintegrated. I shall defy

To the last of my days Blake's puritanical
cleaving of love. Water and stone, mud
and blood, love is strong in the clearing

And in the chorus, a harmony across the whole range
at which time hesitates, and comes to a sudden and
unexpected halt. The song was sung, a hawk hung

Over the centre of a vacated space, a turning
circle or record of love's defeat, where time
stayed and built a nest of inalienable experience.

We built an enclosure around it, a bank
to ring it in earth, a ditch to ring it in sky,
with an entrance and an exit, and a night bell

So that it stayed, for time was exhausted
and slept as music. In all the harm a clearing
which would always be there, and always open.

I made all this up. Does it bear a resemblance
to any known reality? Did not the dead prince command
a certain stillness at the heart of an empty space?

A peace-making stillness. An absence of question,
an eye closed on sequence, θυμέλι, the inner protection
against theatre. For something had been lived here,

A bolt of grief, a shout of love, something that
opened the world and was forgotten, a clod of mud
sinking out of sight, but maintaining its plea,

Le Tombeau de Mesdemoiselles de Visée at which
there is a great falling of small sharp pieces
begging to be erased. The changes fall together

Into the pit and, listen, the spirit is moving now,
a trance music that ripens under the silence
and says to the darkness Hold back your strides

Until these powers are matched and finally free.
Or as Beryl said observing Nina Simone's way of taking her bow
and striding off the stage, That totally uncompromising woman.

Studies in the reconciliation of world and fate
wrapped up and placed at the centre.
Take your bow and stride off-stage.

RALPH HAWKINS
Swirl

Go back, return
I have a myriad of different thoughts, colours
astronaut, plumber, farmer and mail man
start again never ends
the closing rain sounds like soil
scattered on a box   of
an oak with many limbs
to become   after a long pause
an investigative buddhist
banana leaf flower imprint
sobre vestido y falda
tumbling and fumbling through
the great all of it
like a scratchy old film
trying to keep a hat on in a force nine
an image of a communal kitchen, Petrograd
and all those Bolsheviki
in those early days smiling
heady with it all
with that possibility   still

I'll Never Get

you don't love me, he, him
the exception shows up
we watch the blue planet
fart, tart and heart
he was lucky to live
I gave him mouse to mouse
you'll get over it, you always
ride your pony, get on your
I felt my heart race
in mental space
unexpectedly we took the corner too fast
I know it's a two-way thing
plug and socket
when you shut the door the world flickered
whose voice is that
fog horn
milan sausage or hamburger
it's in his kiss

REBECCA TAMÁS
Witch Sister

a sort of woman's face
all gods in it
dearest sister
dearest beloved
marriage comes as knife between us —
we don't need it

witch sister
passionate head and arms
excellent culottes

the way to breed magic is to put our heads together
for now the new epoch appears
passionate cheek and foot
where are our 2000 years?
where are our state institutions?
where are our languages
heavy and graphic on the walls?
giant churches and pyramids glitter
in a weird unholy air
as we stand there brazenly
rubbing our stomachs and laughing   like dogs

yes explosions are good
mountains coming down like pebbles
bridges yawning off into the void
but also

we take each other's hands
our hair turns to snakes
terrible terrible
and it begins

JOE DUNTHORNE
Another Poem Beginning with a Line from Proverbs

Those who flatter their neighbours
are well-liked by their neighbours is how
I think it goes.

Mine are in Jerusalem.
I feed their cat the jellied salmon
and with just this rhyme

I am with them at the wall
that wails though that could be my newborn
wondering where I've gone.

Do you ever feel like God
with a copy of everyone's keys?
The cat makes a lemniscate

between my knees. What even *is* time?
What even sleep? I put myself down
on their hallway's rush matting.

> (Jerusalem has a syndrome.
> Paris has one too; tourists go insane
> from all the people not in love.)

And when I wake the weave has left a pattern
on my cheek — *look* —
I think I see a man's face in it:

the simmering eyes, the neck coming out
in maps. The messiah and all the allergies
he transcendently ignores.

Oh yes, I'd love to run away with him
to Stockholm.

LISA SAMUELS
Each day I take a different path

After Denise Riley after Friedrich Hölderlin

the other instinct
gravels my chest against the air
I mean to open the chest
to have more a target
revelry in the window
like a tumult

how can blind celerity
cuss so fast the
topic streaks behind?
I mean it's only breakfast and
my credence clearly

plush notes on the door
from which beside there'll
be a testimony quiet shout
open the door yell
like to accept

the made-up multi-part
fabric of the real
like it's made of
dense sheen hair

like kowhai blossom bells
entwined with kitchen flanks
like endoderm inhaling
what's called meaning
that rolled near against

the touch's electric
fences in the dark
apparent outward shrieve
the mark makes too
curled a wish to

know to say
we make time for
each other hurry blossom
fast ilk out toward
the passant glimpse a
plummet on the street

MEGHAN PURVIS
The Wych Elm

The tree stands full of starlings, grooves around its base
where cats scratch and foul the earth, furious
the bark won't hold them when they climb.
A lost parakeet dawdles in the lower branches,
a flash of yellow feathers invisible as night comes.

I could join them — could put my hands to swollen knots
shaped as if meant for my palms, throw my shoes in the river
and climb to the tree's first broad split, slip warm-bodied
into its hollow trunk. As if its wood was so much party-dress,
as if anything like taffeta could stop my mouth.

ANDREW SPRAGG
after :: all

there are lines left to learn
or thinking of it all

there under the gaze
of our unmerited attention

in the shimmering
dray age where there were

curds and contemporary
songs sung

so much and so many
after and in the usual fashion

we appear as a shock of
luck or like it

stepping from our own fretful
wreckage or pressing on

after
        all

there are some days with so much
suffering or rich complaint

that there is the sweet stuff
where all states are

frozen and by moments
it would let your

self tick out of motion
hammering into the sweet

set — ash piled by leaves and
melancholy as a pool

by turns too
shallow or deep

to be all a pool
and this to be it yet

after
          all

life friends is a stoppered
mechanism — after some intoning

few thoughts spoiling
for all horizons

TOM LOWENSTEIN
By the Bridge at Uji

Poems for Denise

Of all the directions in which
the bridge could lead us,
there is just one which has been
built in, offering the illusion of simplicity.
So gratefully, we'll take this.

*

Some people I know cross light-heartedly
and disdain to make a fuss. There are others
for whom a direct line to the other side
represents the ultimate labyrinth.

*

In which connection there can only
be a shameful solitude. Nobody is
going to empathise with a trajectory
which appears so fatuously simple
but which opens an almighty gulf.

*

There are certain damselflies whose
wing pattern you absorb only once
they have emerged from the shadow
of the arches where they'd sheltered.

They are weak but valiant creatures.
And I identify with them thus
Without their acknowledgement.

*

Shakespeare, given that it is a
projection of the imagination,
has traversed the bridge.
Metaphorically at least. This
is where fools all caper with
their songs. And dispense crazy
wisdom to the earnest.

*

'The floating bridge of dreams'
is what Murasaki called it. Perhaps
on the one hand the bridge is part
of the river. On the other, among several,
to speak of this and that side represents
a comfortable illusion.
                              Never fear.
We must make the attempt anyway.
Or perhaps she was writing
about an underside reflection
that amalgated one illusion with another.

*

Every step I take on the bridge
and even as I attempt escaping it
proclaims the assumption
that personally I matter. All life forms
require space in which to express
themselves without exclusion
or obliteration of the other.
Thus the way forward remains
conditioned by ambiguity.

*

A bronze statue of Murasaki
stands at the near edge of the bridge.
She's incapable of moving. This
is probably the easiest way
to get across. But she has
no desire to do so.

*

Finding the beautiful in
simplicity. Thus language is
made redundant and we crave
silence to comprehend this.

*

Perpetual motion for
a relatively short period
is a fate we share.

To get stuck is a misfortune. But
even that may be part of the continuity.

*

Gratefully, clumsily, I embrace
the emptiness I come from
and to which like everything
and everyone I shall return.

A companionship of nescience,
neither pleasant nor otherwise.

*

Now in recovery from a remote seeming
head injury, I am in a condition to weep.

And while the world does not require
my pity, the *lacrimae rerum* of universal
existence is more contingent
than when my head was filled
with what I imagined to be significant.

*

Lacrimae rerum. The tears
of things. Or tears inherent.

But there is no psychologist
to explain to us whether
the weeping is intrinsic
but withheld, or if the same
phenomena provoke in us
a lacrimose reaction and
that this represents
a psychological projection.

ROD MENGHAM
Dream for Mahvash Sabet

I sensed in the darkness it didn't matter
The hands keep moving in the old ways
Words and phrases closing round
Like flies drowning in ink
Miles from the desk on which
The decree is written in seconds
In a hundred ways real and imagined
I was drowning without knowing
A vessel with no port to enter
No bridge to span the dark channel

Which fragments of the self are left
When the sails are ripped, and the decks smashed
These are mere keepsakes
When the tides are far away

I remember the room like a dark lantern
Apart from a thicket of distant lights
That glow then vanish

Is this what it feels like to
Orbit a smaller version of the self
Feet caked with the dust of no roads
Upper jaw in pain
Is this what pulls me back to earth
All stays and attachments
From the reddening fire to
The longing to be kept out of harm's way
Perhaps this is the launch-site

The room looks bigger on an empty stomach
And the soft weightless layers of Spring
Demand a forbidden dusting of ash
And the part of me that wants the desert
And the desert wind to smooth the way
Begins to fade too fast to recover

We are all under the same roof
Wings folded and next in line — for ever.

TIM ATKINS
76 Emperor Gotoba

I ate
the rice
which would
bind us
together for
eternity
why
did I
eat the
rice?

ALEX HOUEN
Theory of Flight

After Muriel Rukeyser

No point looking up to the Palermo sky
    for feedback   that explosion of shrieking leaves
in the Botanical Gardens was parrots and I
    am still in them here in the awful Airbnb

apartment where the owner I've not met
    makes Picasso and Einstein and Tarantino
and Cobain and a little Cold War jet
    conspire to cancel my flight with frames.

All day I've been hobbling out of step
    beside you like a pigeon. (That's Einstein pitching in
hoping to put relativity to a stop.)
    I've been walking with one of my father's feet.

You're already up in the air
    heading home   Picasso's *Flying Dove*
though you've started signing off with bear
    head emoji to me as horse head.

Tarantino is that you? I know what to do
    with the heads in bed but not your hearts.
Each time we touch I love how you
    divide parabolas into true arcs

and make me a special restraining harness
    set in the present to remain squarely
in the middle of the air beating our darkness
    into your skin and laughter.   So why

do I stay outside it   keep starting as energy
    and ending as information?   In the Gardens
we marvelled at *Ficus altissima* fig trees
    growing into elegies about their hosts.

Starting as an epiphyte often up a palm tree
    they cast down roots to the ground which grow
over time to support the fig independently.
    Or they grow in the crevice of a rock or a man

made structure as a lithophyte. Their spreading crown
    grows to a hundred feet. The bark
is smooth and grey with small pale brown
    pustules. Their twigs are hairy and green when young.

The leaves are alternate   ovate to elliptic
    on short stalks with sheaving stipules.
Their flowers are solitary or paired as diptych
    in the axils of the leaves.   *Ficus altissima*

is one of the many trees that hosts lac
    insects (from the superfamily *Coccoidea*)
from which we make the dye lac
    and shellac. I guess they can't fly   they are scale

bugs. In Florida the figs (plus their lacs?)
    are gradually exploding thanks to the *Eupristina*
wasps that pollinate them. They look jet black
    on Google Images.   Look at them tearing into sky.

Kurt Cobain is that you?
Let me know when we're through

NIGEL WHEALE
When Freyr took you

There above, on the trance, the narrow defile
traverse the ice shoulder, the cold spathe
unknow yourself in the hoodings of night

The incident path is strictly yours
a light lance thrown unerringly at the eye's heart
your bright trace alone, hurled from Hoy High

Stimmung on the radio interbreathes
with the alarm-harsh call of curlew over
nowt bield, horse beul, byre under hemel

Mist harl over the blank face of bay at evening
the moon's rim could not be more slight
and the birds really giving out

You taste again the firstness of things for
the nature that is in us is nature already
in social and economic refraction

Letter to Denise at 3am

It seems to be a question less
of copying a style or mimicking
than of a search, or being shown
a way to fit the dream.

Which wakes me up at 3.36am
— *'I haven't got off lightly,*
but I got off' — It dogs me
through my days and every night
          it's different.

Friends buckle our armour,
my friend had said.   He had
lightning under his skin,
fuses for veins. *They hand us*
our weapons, they show us who we are.

I turned to him.   But armour
becomes an opaque pool,
dull reflection rippling in rushlight,
outside time, only
mirror of the dream.   He was
looking for himself,
not me. No wonder I couldn't see.

Friends ripple too, of course,
        and disappear.

Convex, impossible. There's no
self-portrait there but just a dead metaphor
to hold the door for me,
the orphan child of him and you
                        — *plain*
sight goes blind through chasing clarity —

writing in the dark
light of a tiny orange lamp,
in the most small hours,
a mile below the surface.

Visiting Isaac Watts

In Abney Park Cemetery
near the statue of Isaac Watts
who's stood so tall and so benign
for over 150 years, I got
stuck into an interview on my phone:
Denise Riley on death and time
— the way dead language thrives on one
and the other comes to life in rhyme.

And how the boxy shape that Watts
fitted to his hymns
constrains and deepens feeling. This
is our religion, now. The winter sun
had not yet set. The sky was pink.
The path was dry, with dogs. I put
my phone away and went to see him.

SIMON PERRIL
Hollowed be Thy Name

For Denise Riley

Hollowed be thy name
for the back-chat and horror-fuss
blast out the cave mouth

and the pyroticians have left
to squat in fresher crime scenes
rehearsing outrage in agonistic octaves.

So that leaves the mouth,
its thinking lungs creaking and flexing
under paper housing

the moving and the mute objects
we can be when the body speaks
sending out its phantom limb

in tracts led by eyes, hands
and resting heads
shaking from their statuary

yet touching somehow
in the white tent left
joining, cajoling.

I watch Marker catch
a grin without a cat
and focus upon hands

fragile then severed. Why.
Sometimes. Do images. Begin
to tremble?

Hollowed be thy name
for there is song
caught in the small wrongs

ungainly, unkempt, undone
unslung from the holster
centre-face.

Hollowed be thy name
for the vacation I takes
packing for space

to cross borders
faking papers forwards
and towards you.

ROSMARIE WALDROP
Velocity But No Location

There is pleasure in composition, in grasping the connection of the one and the many. The way we gradually discover how the dancer's movements are anchored in, and anchor, the axis she spins around, the way the backbone is held up by the muscles acting in concert; or our sense of self, by the mirror. Without it we are forced into constant activity to make up for the lacking image. Like the squid or dogfish, being heavier than water, must swim continually throughout their lives. Desperate activity, I say, and often fruitless, all brains incessantly active, down into our dreams, leaves off the fever tree, electric.

KEITH WALDROP
Theme

we are differently
tuned

like violin and piano

(listen)

our variations

.

EMILY CRITCHLEY
The Lesson

Cambridge, 2004

1
The backdrop was a secret
secret blue. There had been no
physical rain for ages illuminating
the pleasantness of the year
's flowers. There they still were
however waving. Even if far away
and in shadow. Even if you couldn't tell
them; the reason for which was
quite moving. And could always have
been read a different way. Any
way my reading you about it now
doesn't make it any less amazing.

2

Learn to love yourself, she said, & fuck them. Footstep
in the hallway, shadows echoing. Take hold my palm

& drag me there. Even the one that thinks so far.
I won't make it alone, I said. Retracing my steps,

the lost breadcrumbs. What country made you. Love
does like that, if you let it, tho' sometimes

too recalls difference. Some god can tell the rest,
she said, there's no more why or less. Just have to press on

through intent, each reported sentiment. The air, I said,
might start getting lean. Just have to fall into it, toward

land, like the sea lets it. Formed by your own
hands. And that way is it, I said. Heart-felt or flooded.

For Denise, on her birthday

was it Ewan's lipstick
in the corner of the dark
blue pamphlet in my heart
well that'll do the trick
the direct line
along the spine to
London & then north
to Cambridge or the lane
past UEA to Yorkshire
then the longer prospects of all
the pictures you know the ones
in other people's houses or
wherever the galleries store
the current unselected staffed
by those who find it hard to park
& switch off the car radio
echoes with our passions
& we step back out
on wooden steps
that lead up to a cloudless sky
the top one loose

man mohammed

folders with a yellow edge and one with a red
into it went my passport behind a desk i could see
the key for the toilet on a plank of wood handed to a man
when will we be seen and by whom what will we say there is no one
to vouch for us how do we prove ourselves what's the simplest way of
    speaking
to be understood immediately without ambiguity should i look in the
    eye should i
raise the tone of my voice queer it defy expectation to lessen suspicion
everything following the body i could say i eat a lot although i am
    weedy
where my first boyfriend feasted i am dun although my father passed
for white he says when he and my mother moved to their first house in
    england
the neighbour opposite called a friend to ask what indians were like
the neighbour tells my father this after thirty years
after my mother and father watch peter sellers in the party
and say that's exactly how indians used to dance back then
my mother hides in the quietest room in the house speaks in her
    loudest voice
lines to india unclear her family as close as the telephone
the midwife tells her after having children your race and my race lose
    their shape
we her kids sit in front of the television betray urdu with english
we want to pray with our mother in her bedroom and can't help
    knocking
the electric heater laughing each of us sitting on our feet trampling
    the silence
where are you from my history teacher asked he went round the class
what religion there are very few muslims left now in india
he wrote of me i am a fly bashing from here to there in my chair
i am a squirrel come back from the gym face deflated arms askew
i want someone to sit and listen to without having to contribute

not the surgeon who rolls in the patient saying i want to do this one
    first so i can go
i am the anaesthetist prioritising no
can i nip to the toilet what if i go and they call my name
what if they find the man mohammed in the red who can't be found
what if boo to a goose what if the tip of a billion
why needs vouch you will be mistaken

LYN HEJINIAN
A Visitors' Book / Passage of Time

For Denise Riley

Then I stopped writing.

And colored marbles like clenched teeth in a glass bowl serve as the
centerpiece on the dinner table.

Later I start writing to invent an upright robin on exterior bitten
ground.

Then I hear the low mumbling to himself of a somnolent dog the
color of an overcast sky on the other side of a sagging wooden
fence.

Proliferative, incendiary, struggling — these are positive values,
but so too are: bovine, generous, calm.

Almost, but not every, person has hips; how many do you have, dear
reader, and are you incendiary or bovine as you ride them?

Presumably, though it's hard to be certain since the principal figures
are murkily portrayed, they are men taking a chance out from
under a stand of trees.

It seems that maternal fulfillment is timeless.

Some say the soul is a mechanism for processing impressions,
acquiring impressions, producing thoughts.

How very different are water-borne idiocy, crepuscular rag rugs,
a fungus ring in a forest?

The conscious mind can have a strong impression of blind windows on a blank wall, or of acidic sycamores, or of goldfish gasping in wine, or of bodies scurrying, heaving, swaying through the city.

I abandoned the idea of writing a chapter on ubiquity, then I thought of writing a chapter on propinquity, but the presence of iniquity has prevented that.

Depressed by mere cleverness — my own — I stopped writing again.

The poet of the past will avoid simplistic interpretations of the future and dependence on meter as the sonic landscape swells with sound.

I begin again in narrow daylight and again in broad dark.

You do so too, mingling with others who enjoy a beautiful, lasting color which is an enigma of the heart.

IMOGEN CASSELS
A reportage on moss

which is like fur or furze. I would pin like a heartflake our once path
   down the valley / I was sick as a dead bird brightened by the sense
of promises coming true — onto this landscape.   small flowerless.
   it is like a park, then a sea, then a heaven. may you conduct water
in sleep — and in your mercy hear our prayer.   which in summer
lies in the light like you til nine, or new august. happy unsubjects
   to fate. wooddiscolouration — clearwater. the moss is unlike pine or
fir-oils, just poor. it does not wake   dewy skin is the new boy
down the road; eye-green like a sternum.   which is similar to anything /
even the dent of a baby's head   my bright daughter you can't see.
when I am married let me wear sphagnum at my temples   peat-moss
 which braids itself like ferns. moss like the heather when you died
like deep honeysmoke. my laurels without you are tiny now.   and at
each end, darkening, you, moss, stretching out like   a   day

: the practice of liking in order to be like/d
: a qualifier; a verbal characteristic of performative femininity

"Do I like that you, like, liked my post?"

likeless, adj. *obs* > unlike; unequal
"Vn-like manige and likeles" (*Genesis & Exodus*, a1325)
[Jacob sorts the sheep from the goats]

*

like, from Old German *līko* — body (originally appearance, form)
Do you, like, like my, like, like, like that?

*

unlike = *informe*

*

I Like, Like the Way
Can We Just, Like, Get Over

: choice feminism
: predication on preference // eradication of systems

*

Personal Essay on Upspeak - I Like, Like the Way I Speak
www.elle.com/life-love/news/a30443/i-like-my-upspeak/ ▾
14 Sep 2015 - And, like, so should you? ... I'm not big on **upspeak**, nor much of a vocal
fryer, but I do occasionally lower my already-throaty register for that ...

The unstoppable march of the upward inflection? - BBC News
www.bbc.co.uk/news/magazine-28708526 ▾
11 Aug 2014 - Whether it's called the upward inflection, high-rising terminal or simply
"uptalk", the habit of making statements sound **like** questions is a ...

From Upspeak To Vocal Fry: Are We 'Policing' Young ... - NPR
www.npr.org/.../from-**upspeak**-to-vocal-fry-are-we-policing-young-women...
23 Jul 2015 - Women get policed more often for "vocal fry" and "**upspeak**" than their i ...
I remember one in particular said I sounded **like** "a valley girl and a ...

Speech quirks upspeak and vocal fry can hurt your ...
www.businessinsider.com/**upspeak**-vocal-fry-hurt-your-reputation-2015-7 ▾
3 Aug 2015 - You're probably familiar with **upspeak**? **Like** when someone's voice goes
up at the end of a sentence, even though they're not asking a ...

What is Upspeak? - YouTube

https://www.youtube.com/watch?v=2RjPOUZkLfU
25 Jun 2013 - Uploaded by Patrick Muñoz
When simple statements all begin to sound **like** questions, our
authority and confidence as speakers begins to ...

Can We Just, Like, Get Over the Way Women Talk? -- The Cut
nymag.com/thecut/.../can-we-just-**like**-get-over-the-way-women-talk.htm... ▾
9 Jul 2015 - **Like**, have you ever noticed that women apologize too much? ... professor,
women who suffer from **upspeak** — also known as "Valley Girl lift"?

*

"Does the soul have a sex? Or does sexed being confine itself to the body, and if so, is there a permanent risk that it may seep through into the neutral soul? The Homeric psyche was a faint and squeaking ghost, an asexual bat-like thing. It would be a thousand pities if women wrote like men, or lived like men, or looked like men, for if the two sexes are quite inadequate, considering the vastness and variety of the world, how should we manage with one only? Ought not education to bring a sex, the swaying in and out of it is more like ventures among descriptions than like returns to a founding sexed condition. (Denise Riley, *Am I That Name*, 24; 64; 28/Google Books)

"To whom do I owe the power behind my voice, what strength I have become, yeasting up like sudden blood from under the bruised skin's blister?

My father leaves his psychic print upon me, silent, intense, and unforgiving. But his is a distant lightning. Images of women flaming like torches adorn and define the borders of my journey, stand like dykes between me and the chaos. It is the images of women, kind and cruel, that lead me home." (Audre Lorde, *Zami: A New Spelling of My Name*, 3)

*

JAMES CUMMINS
A Chorus

that loss left a burning wind upon the early dusk
sooner or later the road straightens and all eyes look skyward
where belonging meets memory lost in the longing without returning
                                                                    home
evening breeches the room with shades of ochre and sits — stillness
eyeing the movements tenderly
from that little plot
voices trapped on magnetic reels
turning poles
if ours were reversed would you crawl through the years
turning tales and would the reaction be the same
splitting the bark and branch watching the river rise
that quarter acre high above the sky
becoming a part song
to be sung — a chorus

upon inducing stage three general anaesthesia the incisions were
made just below the hairline and so establishing a posterior margin
on the temporal lobe abnormal tissue from both the left and right was
tenderly excised to control the intractable epileptic seizures at the cost
of amnesia excepting continuously apprehended conscious awareness
as in primary memory that is the shallow angle sunlight touching
thin filaments around the window frames mistaken for rain or mud
fire statuettes casting curiously anodyne figures on cheap net curtain
frills or flailing a feather boa as in dancers with prosthetic limbs
replacing an absence after injuries the brain utilizes the exo-brain to
outsource its memory for improved functionality during the days after
non-restorative jagged sleep as in inserting fresh infeeds to multiuser
dungeons with multiple dimensions for our entire topography to
revolve around always ground against another on its own conversely
the torque continues as never nothing.

KYLE LOVELL
Midleaflight

Caught that half-volley as carapace,
in a versicle that's bright green, or an altar placed icon
that burns and grasps and wanes.

A leaf in mid-sight from that moving window
of a peat-laden land; this goodbye
is as useful as oil, or the way that land lies.

Draws back and forth against the move-
ment of a river that hooks itself with wild
brown trout, all silted and bitter.

These moments of breath, they all bring
brack in celebration of flow and matrimonial bonds,
something we — or *I* — wish we could agree upon.

But now, here and now, is not
then, or then the gravity of love lags behind
these smiles and tongued almond graftings.

It's a bottle of what might have been in time,
and yet time catches itself as an ill-
timed cough, and stifles that movement.

ADAM PIETTE
Fiveways

For Denise Riley

i

market strangulation forcing
scored fraught intensities
sidelines tyremarked through to
and you clean thoroughfared
in margolene & thrumming signs

ii

and she told me you're free to go
as long as you listen to what I have to say now
you sigh and say you understand but do you
darling do you
sometimes I wake and stare at nothing in the dark
& that's where you are

iii

in the eye a beam
at the door a shadow woman and wolf
its eye a nest of arrows
circle of fire at the rim of the earth
a comet or streak of light on eyelid
five lights on my bike

iv

she sang in a wave of sound
her timing a loving measure
singing and sighing a lovesong
all on a winter's day
to the air the cold air
to the dark and frozen air

v

I scramble sometimes to the tops
of hills to see what views there are
the views of famous beauty spots
though you might find the rubbish tips
rather strange choices high up here
the strewn earth thick with gulls and rats

vi

wait for words with strained ear
wait for voice in the dark
wait for sights on the screen
wait for beats on the pulse
wait for the drama of it to come
all just all for you

GEOFF WARD
Ine Eruptions

It doesn't look a bit like what it isn't,
And you won't know for sure what time it is
When every aspiration turns to byzant-
Ine eruptions of a sign that isn't his

Or hers, or mine, or any kind of omen
(Deriving from the Latin for 'a fold')
That might be scrawled like *This Way to the Gnomon*
Across the sky in contrail or be sold

In bulk in dreams. Your tiny hand is frozen,
But I don't want to clasp what might dissolve;
This glove is made of sodium. A Zen
Monk, scrabbling for a koan to resolve

Abruptly hears the sound of one foot clapping,
But not in my back yard. Hears distance laugh
The whole nine yards, the squawk of gulls, waves slapping
The seaweed on the jetty at Loch Tarff.

Pantoum

The sculptor is known for his moon-shapes and use of the organic
He invites us for the weekend to his white house on the Lizard
Harsh words are exchanged and he chases us, brandishing driftwood
We decide we hate modernism and that life is good in Cheam

He invites us for the weekend to his white house on the Lizard
Where I noticed my eyes had changed colour in the cold
We decide we hate modernism and that life is good in Cheam
Despite the steep increase in barely solved murders

Where I noticed my eyes had changed colour in the cold
The princess was looking for a pea to lend significance
Despite the steep increase in barely solved murders
I found her a warm space and floated immediately

The princess was looking for a pea to lend significance
Here, where men sit and hear each other groan
I found her a warm space and floated immediately
Consult the cards, watch carefully, thin paper for Mao's thoughts

Here, where men sit and hear each other groan
New caves are going up, ready for the managers
Consult the cards, watch carefully, thin paper for Mao's thoughts
Where stands the deserted transmitter: put on goggles

New caves are going up, ready for the managers
He had got to grips with history and thrown it in a corner
Where stands the deserted transmitter: put on goggles
Poring over sheets that bear the legend *Desperate Drenchings*

He had got to grips with history and thrown it in a corner
When he came across his father, for many years north-facing
Poring over sheets that bear the legend *Desperate Drenchings*
And laughing at the government

When he came across his father, for many years north-facing
So as to catch the sunlight, rolling on the sea
And laughing at the government
Of beauty, of loss and of love's mystery

So as to catch the sunlight, rolling on the sea
When I held her I held vines and crumbling balustrades that sighed
Of beauty, of loss and of love's mystery
In the same dream, the same car in the driveway

When I held her I held vines and crumbling balustrades that sighed
The sculptor is known for his moon-shapes and use of the organic
In the same dream, the same car in the driveway
He invites us for the weekend to his white house on the Lizard

STEPHANIE BURT
Pomegranate in a Bowl of Water

1

Am I the jailer, or the girl, or the mom who saves
The girl who cannot be saved? Or am I standing
Not quite patiently before the tiny
Chaos of floating, fibrous tasteless plaster-
Colored bits, like whole days
From a year that you won't
Remember, trying to pick
Out the last few acidic and fructose-bearing
Seeds? Inside my world
Is another world, the color
Of Mars, and inside
This Mars, a honeycomb
Of easily envisioned colonies,
A series of bubbles for humans to hide inside
Or else a broken-open
Cinnabar-scarlet richness, ripe
For bees. All the bits
You would want to eat sink
Slowly towards the bottom of the bowl. You can stain
Your fingers by choosing to taste
The remainder yourself
Or feed them to children, who, being children, asked
Every day for a week,
Then left what we gave them intact on their
Plates. How do we tell
The difference between what such children
Say they want and what we think
That grown-ups need?

2

When I am most
Myself
I feel like a thief

Not so much rich
As sour and sweet

In the story we heard
You can't
Be mother and daughter
At once
It defies
Belief

To taste the seeds
You have
To take a side

Not so much rich
As sour and sweet

Other than those
Who never
Had anything there is no one
In this world or

The next one who can
Say they have
Nothing
To hide

Razor Clams

the water's image in the salted sky
the graduated sky   cloud-daunted sky

like the tessellated moving wedges
clouds entice across the bay

one after another who knows where they go more slowly
than sciomancy led you to believe

like a belief
like the filter the sifter of what you will

believe from what you can imagine
the anxious grains the supersaturated

flesh what you consume
with pleasure is your life

almost open once amniotic
then strenuous and then Lethean now gone

pellucid in saline cold you find
yourself attracted to emptiness

you have already forgotten everything

NATHAN HAMILTON
From *To You Song*

> ... we can argue that the disentanglement of social life from the
> ferocious domination of mathematical exactitude is a poetic task,
> as poetry is language's excess: an insolvent enunciation in the
> face of the symbolic debt.
> —*Franco "Bifo" Berardi*

car park you are calling
come   be a car park

just fill and empty
over days

your siren wind
-slice note   metal edge upright
like an I-

slat of sad
robot song

  harped on architecture

  of aloneness in a city air

*

early birds already are
in the morning
ahead of me bring in the you

so to speak who are you
and who you are
to me is the thing
am just the sum today
of the you i help
for some reason sing

of wishes to be in this place
with you and me in it
to be in it always

one shutter half-
agape to light
the night behind us and far off yet

*

so this to the you
you are the you
yet lost
on other sides of space
we attend
and care without

assignee
we dance in a kitchen
of words   our guts
chatter unusual returns

        free
adjustment intervals against
adverse possession

oh when did it get so expensive
just to sit about

TIFFANY ATKINSON
There is no sexual relation

(*Jacques Lacan*)

And the lime tree flings out such
a thunderhead of seed
  a god is withdrawing o did one of us forget

thy gold thread twitching and thy net of fairy-lights through everything
My fingers come back looped with glitter
  & I look up
  from my little house of paperwork

The lawyer with the sharp teeth like a grade-school devil
  's at his counting desk
  deploying words like *compartmentalise*

Of course desire loves a small enclosure
and its glammy way with surfaces
  I can't help that

I'm just a slow blink in a shaft of light
that plants its jewel in my toadish forehead
  Well
  was I ever a woman of sound sense

It's my turn to speak I think
  I'll tell them I'm not in today
& fold myself down in the ticklish grass Yes

see my pale hand spring out and my tacky tongue
  that flickers on the quick &
  slippy ling o

CALEB KLACES
The sensitive period

> All hindsight shakes itself out vigorously like a wet dog.
>   —*Denise Riley, 'Silent did depart'*

The lake is here to support the falling light.
The pale blue pleasure-boat is here to slip towards the small horizon.
The inflatable vodka luge is here for happy hour.
The infant is here to learn to appreciate landscapes.
The dog is here to chew the surface of the lake.

The factory supplies the lake with a pink streak of chemical effluent,
    here to provide local jobs and use up the father's pot of cadmium red.
The boat's wake is here to reconcile the chemical pink with the
    reflected auburn flare of late sunlight.
The young teacher walks through loosened light to relieve himself
    of the day.
The patient runs towards him, away from the holy water.
The off-duty ship mechanic is below deck to criticise the barman's
    pouring angle.

The electric light below deck is increasingly soulful.
The captain is here to imagine ways the sunset could sour.
The use of multiple vanishing points: the effect it might have on
    passengers.
Points vanish into waves and waves into points because the father is
    familiar with the photon.
The amateur photographer is here to avoid introspection.

The retired triathlete is here to rescue the three-legged dog from
    polluted
    water.
The inflatable luge is here to rescue the retired triathlete.
The infant's ice cream is here to melt into the eczema on the wet dog's
    muzzle.
The stag party is here because who else will sing in praise of the
    sunset.
The climber has stepped off the mountains in fear not of darkness but
    its
    onset.

The infant is here to appreciate everything her mother has given up.
The mountains rise up to resist the earth's turn.
High in the futile mountains, the purpose of the suddenly dense grey
    cloud is unclear, nor is the father sure he is responsible.
The actors are here to popularise the bar. Time is marked by the fading
    of the actors' talent.
Shafts of light broach the subject of the lake with the father.

Passengers scramble for the heat of returning care.
The new, weak care has no width or height.
A thin covering of heavier care helps reconcile the boat's movement
    with
    its mass.
The beard hairs stuck in the foreground pines are here to show the
    father's long-sightedness.
The new, weak, stiff, yellow care is here to remind the teacher of the
    armpits of his cheap shirt.

The cheap shirt is here to expose the working conditions inside the
    factory.
At last, the father leaves the sunlight alone.
On the cobbles the prostitute wobbles to prove the sun has gone down.
The streetlights are lit to show who lights the streetlights.
The scene is flung upwards, and comes down grayscale.

Grainy shadows bring depth to the patient's restrained body.

The doctor imagines the patient's great effort not to be aroused by her own body.

The long blonde hairs from the father's head, curling in the pine trees, are here to remind him he is also inside the scene.

The body gets everywhere.

The infant rearranges the words to make a different father.

SAM BUCHAN-WATTS
Gigha

the ear instructs the eye to wade out with sound,
long legs without waders give thanks
listening to sounds lost to the mingling of water

which makes them. Rhymes etched on the waves
each time they subside, 'unique & miraculous',
the water strides out from its shores in great hoops.

JOHN WELCH
Late

October, the year's late sunlight
Is stalking the ground.
Slanting through branches
How far the light reaches in
And the trees, their stilted performance.

A sense of baffled expectation,
Is this what weighs the branches down?
It almost reaches to where you are
An infant again,
The puzzle of itself being awake,

An echo being the sound you make
Finding yourself over here
In the realm of the almost forgotten.

Draining the pool of its silence.
On a day of triumphant stillness
Enough is almost too much, and now these
Late-flowering peaceful torments?

Still learning to be here,
This 'you'. It is a silence inside me.
Caught in its bubble of breath.

ANNA SELBY
Wildling

I had to rupture
when I stopped being a child
until a panther birthed out,
dashed itself forward —
the water leaping — a frightened crowd
rearing open to my legs.
My breath, my heart, my chest,

shrieked.
I let them hear. Shook them,
silenced the never-never-always in my ear,
fractured the ice sheets
that stoppered me all those years.
I lead my wandering body back
to the waves. From them
burst a wild, wild, howling creature.

MARTIN THOM
From *Growth and Form, or Erysichthon and Mestra*

vii

As kettledrums, trombones in ocean call on harps of rain
    To send glissandi skittering from heights of mountain snow;
    As fire fed rounds upon itself and calls for wood again;
    Gourdsmen run to store and pen, since *cibus omnis in illo*
    Causa cibi est, and this from Ovid be rendered so:
    'All his chow's the cause of chow', until division wind
    The loaf back to the grain again, until partition slow
    The catenary of the air that Zeno's bow defines
As beauty rare by gravity on D'Arcy Thompson's watchchain shines.

viii

The riches of the palace gone, from things Erysichthon
    To persons switched, to Mestra footloose on the sand,
    Who, in fear of mastery, called in her sea debt from the foam
    And changed her face and clothing to be an outright fisherman.
    With hook, line and sinker, delighted by the strand
    And by her prints that in oblivion faded out and fell
    The daughter duped Erysichthon, whom arts of change outran
    As to her vase restored and with a dolphin on the swell
She generous to his fault herself as mare as cow as deer did sell.

At dusk to the crossroads that *most cursed keytife* went
    To drum against the final wolf upon his begging bowl
    And once the bridewealth of the brine was counted out and spent
    He fed himself straight to himself, in savage mind and soul.
    Mestra's vase was into Pyrrha by the current gently rolled
    As through that thoughtful tenagos the fishers hauled their nets
    And Aristotle at the jetty watched the timeless tale unfold
    Of the household of the world, of excess and of defect
In forms that grow beneath the heavens and differ in their mortal dress.

BEN BOREK
The School of Biological Realism

Eurasian hooded crow. Grey mantle. Freighted subject.
Chestnut bombing as I cycle past
a solidarity of civic allotments.
A frog hops between them. Flashing the crow
what may have been a smile
with what may have been coy teeth.

My bicycle is called Hercules, my office complex — Mordor.
My breath is not a dragon's. It sets in front of my head,
then my labouring cuts through it. I prepare each day
to persuade the innocent of Mitteleuropa
of the benefits of electric toothbrushes or mobile phones
or batteries or vitamins or granulated 'espresso'.

Round the workshop table it was agreed:
freighted nature. Tread gentle on taxonomy.
See that goldfish bowl? That's me in my scholarly cups,
earnest and tremulous, trudging through mulch
to the brutalist campus where semester is wide open.

Now East Anglian autumn turns Eurasian.
Metallic light is still metallic light, but the burnishing is different.
I am east of the Oder. I see a private doctor.
I've been feeling a little equinoxal. The cusp of terms.
The leaf-fall month. The leaf-melt season.

With maximum
Politeness
Delicacy
Tact
You helped us all agree
The Domestic Lyric is to be avoided

But it is evening in my tenement.
A tram wails past.
I look and see: a Eurasian leaf-red cat.
An allegory of *something* amiable.
A perma-moult; breaking all Linnaean rules.
It eyes the goldfish bowl while, outside, a hooded crow ...

Jabbing tight
this hard worn cold marks
the wind, for keen, draining
slicing here to the east
stopped now
but creeping.
Bright, restricted
looking over
streams rising
two windows
the planes
red dashes and points.
whispered voices
more manly
when startled
and trusted of course.
Its speed
quite wary for
all that groans and
flashes. The place
needs in more
frozen, that out and round
glance settled and
salvage.

SAMUEL SOLOMON
Party Writing

A festschrift is never your party,
though peacocking friends do buoy you along.

I spent a year trying out your ear
and wanting to cry at my party.

"Let's Dance" *did* hammer, whatever
anyone said. Time didn't stop but looped

to the rhythm of the rain that almost
never rains in Southern California.

A lonely listening party, singing back-up
for an imaginary friend (that's where it is!).

I don't know how to write it now,
which implement, in its place, will

chisel out a party writing.
Lapis lazuli might be doubly lapidary

and doubly feminine, like "the social,"
if you carve it with

itself. I'm told it's actually
a rock and not a mineral,

made up mostly of lazurite,
itself dodecahedral.

Now imagine a lazurite curd snack
to freeze, chisel into pieces,

and share, in the early evening,
after sneaking out of a party

through the side door.
We're lying when we're not

about why we have to leave,
(it's good to get some air),

and then coming back in, one by
one. The plan was for one of us

to declaim to the host, in Regency fashion:
"I never promised you a rose garden!"

It's true, but you said it first,
and I repeated it, conspicuous.

TONY LOPEZ
Cartesian Light

At the year's end a comet appeared low in the sky, tail pointing west.
Stroke weights are heavy and only capitals are available.
Lead and other type metals were diverted from their proper use.
You've got to be sensible these days.
A colour looks best when massed and used economically.

In earlier books the initial letters were filled in by hand.
It is a world of propositions that stand in various deductive relations to
    one another.
This staff does not exist.
Written signs are quotation marks for logical thinking.
Later versions were narrower, with fewer sorts, and required less paper.

The forms are clear and correct and elaborated to the smallest detail.
Bands of men plundered farms for supplies.
Writing enables us to build more content into our beliefs.
The curve and the tail of the lower case 'y' have been altered.
Austerity causes dust to rise.

Fellows and students dispersed into the countryside.
Paper and pencil operations occur in the material world.
For a Cartesian light exists in the air, for a Newtonian it comes from the
    sun in six and a half minutes.
Use our resources to see if your idea is original.
It wants to be turned around, opened up, and paged through.

Phlogiston is what we now call hydrogen.
The spine-tailed swift flies faster than any other bird (present
    indicative).
These brackets were made from open-face capital 'O's cut in half.
I come from Colophon, twenty miles northwest of Ephesus.
Alphabetic lines broke through the narrow magical circle.

VAHNI CAPILDEO
She Appears, Pallid, Adamantine and Ablaze

Required we   descend
                          descend
                          descend
into a hall beneath another hall
a royal hall below a royal hall
this hall is jammed tamesis conserve hall

All of myselves   descend
required I   descend
                           descend

Called all all call jarring voices cored to corps
velvet creeps along raked seating coxcombs
velvet aisles stages exits firedoors
velvet outlines lightsout fuchsia burgeons
pushing gelscapes in the ear and my dear
colleagues   they have the money
who are more   they have the money
who is more

                          present
point ones present and point sevens present
and satisfy outnumbering nettles
I pass
I pass   to the back
                          in the dark

I pass

                          in a cut
                          a cloud

a point four

One who is whole ascends the podium
and wisdoms goldly of our expansion:
A book of poems is no different from
a smoothie. You can market a poetry
collection the same way you market
a smoothie.

In such circumstances   She appears
where dangerous nonsense
is spoken

pallid, adamantine and ablaze.

Go check the coatrack for an aegis.
Scry the panelled walls for phantom owls.
Nothing so obscure.
Nothing from the   shrouded fathers' topspin
armoury of judgment-chaser symbols.

Only   a look
only   a word
that withers
into ordinariness until
cold as the edge of a bell
on strike against sounding the tocsin

the air is clear

                        nothing
                        has fallen
                        away

and the air
is cold and clear

Sitting suddenly upright,
you compare gloves
with Her
while She tells you   of death
reminding you
not to stop

                            speaking

LINDA KEMP
suddenly not in writing but written

in the actuary of
figurative speech
the
          lucid
          tongue
switch
& longing
          quite
the
Orphic platitude

                    hardly rare
the hardwired
tilting the
                    specific
washes of over &
                              meta
          -phonical remark
coefficient perhaps &
in loop

          these
          quiet this
          those quiet
          loops

JENNA BUTLER
The Blue Hour

this land sees through you

knows what is broken
before you bring your bones
    limping & freighted

poplar teaches
what it is to live
circumscribed
    thirty years or heart rot
a scattering of daughters
pushing up from the roots

the way frost
prepares the ground
for summer flax
    hunches stones out
    eases the tilth
tells you plainly of
the core of things

earth baring
its scant winter light
its blue curve of marrow

EDMUND HARDY
Gave Up Being Good

For Denise Riley

Looking from a window above it's like an embedding
of acidic yellows, half the dream of one with
the sun in their face > this stormy sunrise, when an image
takes form, *it will die*, the outer snagged in
all 'the life stuff' — inscriptions darker, lighter than mine
in this *selfsame tale*, but tracked as different, determinedly outer
selves, from further outside: she waxed warm,
and step for step fast after him she hied: 'Is there anybody nigh?'
Straight Echo answered, 'I'. Just as every mandate
falls into the gap — speak, speak
again. Not music playing by itself, nor music in my mind saying
it's gonna be alright. I don't want slippages or resistance points, if
the whole red world to come or present baseline
could rename, and become its new name: Did I let it bleed me? Did I
hit back until it bled itself? Neither friend nor enemy
to count all these working hours looking for
a line to shield the honouring of pleasure when we 'could've been
getting down to this — sick — beat.'

FELICITY ALLEN
Colouring in

> It is reasonable to suggest that fair-skinned people are more liable
> to make the weird conceptual leap that allows one to see blank white
> space as a realistic representation of a face ... Watercolour anticipates
> photography in a number of ways (and was somewhat displaced by it):
> use, prestige, availability and, most strikingly, formal properties.
> —*Richard Dyer*[1]

I went to a talk she gave. I watched the way she moved, moved her
body, her grace, her hands, her hands were talking, her face, the
liveliness of her mind and what it did with knowledge as she released
it through her body to the audience. I wanted to make a series of
filmed portraits of people describing someone else. Varese, or Ligeti,
or Stravinsky for M. I wanted to watch her hands create a portrait.

Moving images just create something else, they don't create
a definitive thing at all.

You're creating the illusion that it's momentary.

A watercolour sketch I did represented him on the university website;
an official queried it. Photography orthodox, painting unorthodox.

Painting on the bigger scale gives you a kind of physicality — more,
not expressive, but more, actually the opposite, more analytical of the
surfaces that you're looking at.

Wanting the painter to emerge through my body.

---

1 *White*, Routledge, London and New York, 1997, pp. 111–113.

And actually the way you've represented the face is how my face feels to be.

I got an impression of a sort of physical endeavour, a body as well as the orbs of the eyeballs. The work of holding a brush and making gestures and having your arm at a certain angle and also having to look very intently at the thing, person, who is in front of you.

I couldn't look at painting because it did that thing to my body that the roses just did. It made me feel molecular and sensual and as if I had to paint. She said, You're making me feel as if I have itches all over me.

Actually, being reduced to an object is fabulous because in a way you yourself can wander out of it and you can leave the object, the flesh object to look after itself or, well, just to sit there in its four-square manner.

I heard the blackbird in the garden and she noted the police helicopter: I hate that, she said.

Tiepolo's got the most malicious yellow anywhere, I think it's great.

It was windy but sunny outside. A deep crimson velvet rose leaned towards us, surrounded by acid green jasmine leaves. Green bushes and the espaliered apple tree beyond. Bright pink cistus flowers beside orange-scarlet roses against the silvery grey fence.

It's more to do with the kind of chatting style that you've got, so there is a very rapid half-conscious adaptation to somebody else's mode.

How had I chosen people as sitters? Literally, I said, colour: I look at people's colouring and the colours they wear. That's one reason, among many others.

Something that's both humorous but not very guarded but also serious.

'I was always taught that in watercolour you shouldn't use black.' Do a series of sitters who are all artists giving advice about painting as I paint them.

The presence of them is really hard to pin down because it actually does a meandering as a series.

The racialised adoption policy of the 1970s: for this one human being, a chaotic logic which led to biological, adoptive, and step-parents from different African, Caribbean and British countries, sometimes misattributed, to provide an identity called 'mixed race'; geography as colouring in.

They've got this family likeness you know.

At the Hayward I invited her to contribute to a discussion about Paul Klee and poetry with two other poets with whom there was an odd moment in the green room and I was impressed by her humour and tact. Another sitter once said people want to suck her story out of her; people like you, Mum, who love a family saga. People have warned me against unlocking the identities of the sitters from the portraits. The stories they have shared are inside me. You can occupy me however much you like, but I'm not turning on their stories to gratify your fascination.

It was a night of meteors. We looked at the vivid sky. I can't remember which part of our long conversation over twenty-four hours took place during the sitting. For much of the second picture we were both quiet with exhaustion.

J.T. WELSCH
Franny & Mabel

In the quietest house at the dark end
of the quietest street in the quiet town,
two dogs curl together in sleep.
An hour ago, my sister went out to
the garage to hang herself and Franny,
perched on the mat, her great ears twitching,
turned to ask, 'What will become of us?'
Used to little Franny's questions,
Mabel sighed from the ancient sofa.
'What right have we to safety?'
the wee one asked again,
as the warm June night
stifled a dreamy half-whimper
and held the earth toward peace.

JOHN CLEGG
Dormer Windows

Grid streets in Pardue
Oriented so the sun

May rise on cue in certain
Dormer windows

Are a starmap out of
Kilter with the field lines —

Which justify their own grid
By the gradient

At which cows
Topple in high weather.

Where the grids mesh
Pardue takes priority,

Those fields which abut
Town backlots carve out

Equilateral packages
Of diddly-squat.

Like here. Two cows
Relentlessly chew off the overlay,

Expose the one-
To-one map of the very local.

Houses, being fixed,
Seem transitory:

Impositions on this other grid
Which, though

Imaginary, is our measure
Of the permanent.

Because what can't be filched
Needn't be nailed down.

CARRIE ETTER
Ever Among

> ... to converse with shades, yourself become a shadow.
> —*Denise Riley,* 'Listening for Lost People'

Where the sea bears the colour
of slate. To withdraw, to subdue
my teeming for. Call it an undersong.
The rabbit stilled in plain sight,
on the green: attentive to I
can't know what. Under an oak's
canopy, I try to empty. She is near,
in the rabbit's poise, in the long swathe.
I must and no, cannot.

HARRIET TARLO
Two Cut Flowers for Denise Riley

(i)

the philosopher watches the spectre glide
& flit   fast down Łódź avenue
animate   personages taking to
pavements   closed casements
seal streets   lips, breasts, bellies
illuminate   the romance of your
own   wrapped, aging
hands

(ii)

they got darker than he meant them to
beginning   to bleed into body
portals   into blur with sky maybe
autumn   or going out of art
scene   more than cube
red on red   depth, screen or
frame   could interiorise
internalise

COLIN HERD
? + Fiat

After Introduction to *Poets on Writing*

We tumbled in a weird embrace,
wires, ankles, wiper blades.
It was colder inside than out,
and the ? knew the workings,
the vehicle the tenor, the knock
from under and to the left or
coming up from somewhere else,
a condition. This was what
its rumbling meant, ? said, unlinked
to the moss around the inside frame,
damned fiat, its roof window,
all hippy fur and mud,
all goody-2-problems.
It veered and spun and shimmied.
Branches snagged — "it's
like the beginning of *Misery*",
but ?, with big paws, drew blank,
yawned its padded intensity,
might as well have scratched its eyeball,
"except without the winding
roads and the Champagne."

DERYN REES-JONES
Dark Mirror

> I am a ghost writer for poetry.
> —*Francesca Woodman*

I am eight years old that day
you sit for yourself
naked in a white room
in Provincetown. Your inky self
makes a shadow on the floor.
Then, in a polka dot story
(a booklet), *Here is Francesca*
dressed nicely and smug.
We see her departing,
her back in the polka dot dress,
then her legs, and time. Everything
flattened to fit the paper.

The room frames you, opens you up. Is that
plagiarism — pants stiffened with glue —
needles under the skin —
to take a photograph of something
you've never seen? A glass table
on a dark floor.

Now there you are
in Rome, under another leaden sky.
In New York you're a girl with a fox, or the wolves,
running. You hold a calla lily.
Another day alone
amongst the ruins.

In the beautiful empty
you jump to the paper's end
so that wings tear light,
hang from a lintel.
To be all breasts, hands, fabric,
herringbone! A blast of light
and its encroachments.
You scatter yourself
in space and time.

This afternoon I stand
beside you in my yard:
amongst the digitalis.
My poems, like your pictures,
getting smaller, getting whiter.
Confetti or constellations.
Soon there will just be

small areas of glow.

DAVID HERD
November

For Denise

On a bright cold day
That makes me think of Schuyler
With the birch tree
Across the garden
Anticipating snow
And the traffic
Wrapping sound
So that the morning
Has its music
The lyric
In its gratitude
Speaks
What it might know.

That where the phrase
Breaks
Against the intimacy
Of its angles
Knowing
In its intelligence
What a person might disclose
Of love
In its hesitations
And human solidarity
There
Because you taught us
Is what the lyric
Wants to show.

That as you read to us
In Canterbury
With everybody present
Barely breathing
And standing
And the room
Listening exactly
To where you would go
You spoke
Your poem
And everybody and I
Was with you —
This, Denise,
That night
Was what we wanted you
To know.

En descendant à Saint Ouen, Rouen, on rencontre le jeu ondulant

ASSAT	BFARA	CHALUMEAU	DRUMS	ENGLISH HORN
FAGOTTO	GLOCKENTON	HARP	JEU ERARD	
KERAULOPHONE	LARIGOT	MONTRE	NINETEENTH	OPHICLEIDE
PIFFERO	QUINT	RACKET	SCHLANGENROHR	
TENOROON	UNDA MARIS	VOX ANGELICA	WIENERFLOTE	XYLOPHONE
ZINK	ANTHROPOGLOSSA	BOMBARDE	CINQ	
DIAPASON	ECHO OBOE	FYFE	GEDECKTBOMMER	HAUTBOY
JULA	KOPPEL	LUTE	MAJORBASS	
NACHTHORN	OBOE	PAUKE	QUERFLOTE	REIM
SACKBUT	TWELFTH	UNTERSATZ	VOX HUMANA	
WALDHORN	ZARTGEDECKT	AMOROSA	BASSONELL	CARILLON
DUOPHONE	ENGELSTIMME	TYFFARO	GERMAN GAMBA	
HORNLEIN	JUNFERNREGAL	KINURA	LITICE	MELODIA
NASON	ORLO	PHOCINX	QUINTENBASSREGAL	
SERPENT	TROMBA	VOX EOLIENNE	WEIDENPFEIFE	ZAUBERFLOTE

125

You splatted into smaller and smaller bits
your micro-elements get colonized by product placement
trying to cover the shame.

Dark breakfast.

Yes, sugar; I mean the long history of sugar.
Thick black smoke of the cane trash burning.
Rich land gone entirely for rum and candy.

Shivering, head down,
is there a hope
of finding

home for the living heart of justice
so I am not stealing
every bite I eat?

so that I am not wearing
a weave of bodies crushed, to sleek the cotton
of these clothes?

*

A thing put together pretty well to indicate

a thing filled with the guilt of its genre and the history of speaking
   in lines
           somewhat guileless about how it got here.

It needs to become "it."
Implacable. Unbending. But resilient.
It needs to see that quirk, that turn. It needs
to watch.
It needs to try
walking with legs like wings,
flying out and
holding a camera in her gut.
(Stubbornness.)

That's the need to know, to catalogue, to find.

Every act is an act in the politics of yearning.

*

And also the dog was with me, why am I going
on this journey.

       to write the work of political disaster
       that oil slick will kill what we can't even suspect

things we want
things we love

things we respect,
we identify

with them, or are them.
We hardly knew they were there

but we will miss them.
They are made from us and we are them.

So we are walking onward, and we are walking

with them/inside them/losing them

walking carefully, but sometimes as if mourning.

Skin cannot walk

thru any day

unflayed.

*

Years
with smoke and billows of darkness
shifting so that one is caught in them
no matter which way one goes
and memory becomes too much.

The non- , the overlooked, the sidelined, the marginal, the rejected
who are the semi-powerless, are us, we
the new speaking-the-unspeakable subject
without being able always to speak.
"Moral injury" or PTSD? What is an accurate
    alienation? When something comes
    with its own initials — it is a capsule. A cartouche,
        a hieroglyph, It
        abbreviates. Reduces. How
        then to expand it, to express it?

            The feelings skulk and smoke with rage,
        inside the alphabet, inside the pictograph,
            inside the page.

SARAH HESKETH
I am

I am   sat in our back yard
reading Denise Riley.

In a red dress   I would never
have purchased for myself.

I am not   thinking about the
state of Palestine.   I am not

Georgia O'Keeffe.   No, I am not
any of those women, really.

SARAH HAYDEN
Caught, Dashed

The motive for this was to have been a weighing of the full and the empty: the pursed whistling of *snow graphics* against *jampacked rivers red with thickset fish*. My sole prop: your fanned swatches. But at the podium, tightchest fumbling swapped sweat for pattern and once the specified Dewer set to leaking, there was nothing else for it but to use them. mop, mop.

Here, look with me — .

Violetish stains soak towards unbodied handwriting. Lyrics swell: prickling. Every time that door opens on someone else, the horizon is darker, purpler, and the space you won't domesticate remains *bland, milky*. Mouth mistakes air though the scent has been frozen quite entirely away. Again, again. Suspending symbols, the driest lines *destroy private conversation*. We have no script for this, and so move, a shade behind ourselves, along iced, precisely flattened rails.

& o but if you could just lift
those   *shadows tender clear and neutral*
twice clear of coppery lungs —
there would be a hollow, ready tap.

WANDA O'CONNOR
Pythia's rest

not with oars
sinking into form
unlettered and unrhymed
drawing from the stream which can't be moved
the days in her

denied her daughters
leaving the bursting
run-through,
in this House of Snakes
recover. and with
scooping up
olea europaea, broad-leaved, a place to rest
the forest that quilts her

drawing up from below
and with the old vocalization
and whatever obstructs the passage
that spring up
at points of entry

the fruit in her
an opposite side boils
the Pythia, founder of cities
it having the shape she expected

it is worth hearing
the white-armed one crosses,
toward purchasing
toward a wind that
any heroic heart

but with water, to keep a steady hold on bodies.
of what censures in her
to the assembly place
she did correct her complaint
making an end of held things

only meant to be hoisting up
and yielding to others.
giving answers as if through a beak   *tsíou-tsíou*
with her tongue she does lick them and so they do
waves all around,
a chance at hospitality
part ornament, part meat
quilts her dully

salt-tongued
gathering, weathercasting
like bits of sea bronze
with no beauty in it
threshold songs

fitful in growth
the light fails before it reaches
of streams, cutting into the fruit
literally, 'fireless'

that things may have the appearance of burning.
lathering in earnings
a warmth of marsh
splits.

KIMBERLY CAMPANELLO
Hydrocephalus

> Neither my note nor my critique of it/Will save us one iota.
> I know it. And.
> —*Denise Riley*

Rather than seek surgery descriptions and diagrams
I white knuckle a purple book. Its lines slide
from eyes to lips like tears. Fateful slippage
of the poet's 'I's — a good idea for a time like this?
Who am I to make such talismanic connections?
Where does this book leave me and my niece's
too-big head? A slip of the surgeon's hand and she's
done for. A slight slip and 'you' becomes you. Three slips
in the Creed at Mass this morning — a new translation
since my last attendance — which was when? Which crisis?
We to *I. Born of* to *incarnate. One in Being with*
to *consubstantial with.* Before 2011? No.
My last Mass was no crisis. I was becoming
her godmother. For that act, it's renunciation
and profession. *I do. I do. I do. I do.*
I do. I do. I do. I do. Except I don't.
And now this. The priest anointed her big head.
She must be smarter than the others. We were ignorant
of the waters pressing the backs of her eyes like pennies.
The lines in my purple book hold steady
like a surgical diagram, cherished, never
forgotten if-when it all works. The endoscope
slides between the lobes of not-her brain. A blank-faced
not-her baby in profile, eyes closed. Endoscope placed
just there. No surgeon's hands guiding it. No knuckles
twitching. The lines, straight and clear and true. Just a little
hole to make. To drain. To beckon the body to absorb.

EMILY BERRY

Hymn

> When I fall into the abyss, I go straight into it, head down and heels
> up, and I'm even pleased that I'm falling in just such a humiliating
> position, and for me I find it beautiful. And so in that very shame
> I suddenly begin a hymn.
> —*Dostoyevsky*, The Brothers Karamazov

When one night
distinguished itself
from other nights
I became turbulent
& fell to celebrating
I hung upside down
a great distance
from the favoured
& this was a species
of what you down
there call shame I
was laughing & when
it seemed as though
others misunderstood
my state I felt
compassion surge
through me like
a person changing
from a body
into a rainbow
Thus delivered
my own body solemnly
contorted & I —
suspended — sang

MARIANNE MORRIS
Poor Elephants Poems

You are a poor elephant who aped me
and I am a poor elephant who aped you
and it wasn't even a real elephant to begin with
and I don't know why we're friends.
There I said it.
Here I am brilliantly foreclosing all of the deals
but actually doing the opposite of all that
under the general bracket of 'life's work'
patiently detecting the humus in which
I have been secreted, shiny except from having been
polished with piss instead of whatever
it is that they use to polish trains. I can't even
talk about what the ocean's been doing today,
mimicking an orchestra and the nightclub
happenings of youth, script that won't play,
smiling clouds, absent mermaids inferred through
erumpent achievements of explosive hydrous.
An acorn, a chestnut. Can't help repeating
the things that were said to you in moments
of youth, even as you say them to yourself.
Say them to yourself thinking that all is
understood, that every unconscious
thing said is a thing said
to the sayer in memory so deep and convoluted
it's like birth
remember they invented logic
but how can you, as a listener,
discern between conscious and unconscious
utterance, particularly when neither of those
two things really probably exist anymore.
These informative images do not evoke my
situation, who do they hope to entice?
What do they hope to effect? Hope is

encouraging but when invisible and absent
and no one can find her as she went out just
for a run but ended up at the bottom of the
river, which flooded the highway this after
noon bringing death to our door, it's
hard to see anything but the end.
If I wanted to give myself or this poem
some abstract epithet like 'Beast of Bernini'
I would have to
prove to you
slowly, over
several minutes
and repetitions, how I
am both the fingering structure that
reaches after eternity and
made of white marble, which cannot be pierced,
only caressed from the outside hard panel,
how I am not simply hardened, or softened,
a dance of opposites or forgetfulness,
how I am helpless as the next when
hoping to achieve comfort.
If I wanted to call myself any kind of name at all I would have to
not just paint a picture of two women dancing,
one the width of a wrist, the other
nicely filling out a pair of overalls.
I won't call myself anything,
my feet are too light
driving off
into reality which location I can't
ever seem to get to,
and all of that seems insurmountable now and
I don't trust you, etc. I now regret which
things have brought me to the
headline, 'Why
England Retained the Ashes', nestling alongside
death squads and terror plots and the Vatican.
But luckily the news

is entwined with compatible accomplices
who prefer being in the spotlight to
reading about somebody badly screwing
some other body.
Mounds of leftover feasts fester in vitriol,
clothes fresh from the factory,
for some reason the inclusion of me in its audience
and I'm supposed to a) lap this up b) feel bad about it c)
apologise and d) refrain increasingly from my own
life as if something bigger than us really were —
is there any point to this it's so messy I'm so sorry.

IAN DAVIDSON
Fish Flesh or Fowl (slight return)

Under cloud cover I leant
on the bar, talked about
myself, a subject as
constructed as if there is no
relationship between the words
and anything else as a puffin
turns out to be a guillemot or a
razor bill or a bird is fish for lent.

And what is in the name whether
the short bird puffs to itself at the
speed of its wings or its puffed
out beak, a delicacy and tasting
of the fish it lives on. And the
puffing sound it makes a short
growl or laugh but all these are
unlikely conjecture and based
on insecure grounds.

Language can only take you so far.
Sometimes you have to step out.
Sometimes you have to quieten the
jangle of nerves connect
inside and outside or link skin
to skin. The loose ends of
being alive and waiting
for a connection I went to
the old places and walked
them round again, too
familiar for words.

MICHAEL KINDELLAN
Poem Written While Listening to Denise Riley Read a Poem

The ear that she
cut from my head

And sewed into
the middle of my breast

Hears now no other
heart than hers

RAJIV KRISHNAN
No Show

For Denise Riley

Spoilers first. The acrophonic ox ploughs through poona.
    The turtle-back hills emerge
        under the blue haze of the morning rain:
    sudden spiderdrop.

Fly the unpolished nails, my
    flesh is waiting — no no-fly, autocomplete
        zone here. The surreptitious, suety
    snot on the obscene privates of good
                            neighbours is a power
        of jailbreak carbon.

            At the women station,
    rockspeak. Sudden bluejay for breakfast.
Talking as if also scratching
            elsewhere. The sickle-leaved
            latex skyline appears as the train
    pulls into the station: always a this to landscape here.

People go where their capital has migrated. Lack
        lives latterly as coffin timber. Diurnal jail mud,
    I need gills here. Through the trees, the river glimmers.
The glances of the poor seek
        not alms not alps not not
The eyes darken, I can no longer, not with this
        trilobite invention, take in
            the light of what was.

O mind, make in desire your hometown.
    Night's raccoon eyes outstare
                the quibbling wall.
    Its salted sidewalks of rhetic
fumbling celebrate purposes you will never
        know. Wear the nugatory hard hat:
  no date without basra.

               Under the robust shores
of the supposed sala tree, now there are cannonballs.
      The light-affronting leaves
reveal an occasional involuntary egg, bravura
             diaper change. The seagulls make a perfect
touchdown on the floodlights in LAX.
What do you do with a good leg
    when you have 3 seconds of it?
From the zincy reaches of the world
                   the hair heir to claw
  give the owl its cheesy smell.
On social placenta in bunkie: poets on social support,
      not of the world, but in soup kitchens —
  snowsit on sere leaf, the ur-form of waste.

Through mingent rain, golden showers, erythemal sunlight.
    Take the daisy butter way to Africa.
  Dear heart, draft rash, if you sought
      flaming rock, the names would come
  for heriot. Employee sibyl, sweep quietly
    through things: piercer auger awl gimlet stiletto.

ANDREA BRADY
Set in Stone

For Denise Riley

The word lodged in the cervical spine
where it is smallest and closest to the skull
originally formed from spit and balled
up paper. A cruel word which refused
to look back at the boyish face looking
for recognition as the water froze into a platter,
a congested mirror. And out here in the wintry

dreamscape of feathered ice, of men
capped and ballasted with sticks
for arms where feeling resonates without
chronology, all the words belong
to me: the fancy, the miserable, the hot.
I manage them all and pay
no taxes on the chance that I might lift,
sheer air, out of my crinolines
through the cloud which is this snow,
the cloud which is here and above.

But there is a difference between being frozen
and being petrified. It's a matter
of the one little name that ticks
still, barely perceptible, in my neck;
against that fading dynamite, that deeper wound
down clock, all the other names I've given
myself are the bragging rights
either of us left on the doorstep
of the graven house.

Lately I know this and am glum, but in my sadness
a softness puffs. It changes the limpet shadow
clinging to the spurred bone to a limpid
shade blown over the tufts. Blown off by just
such a voice as this: the voice who loves
these words, the homes you made in them. So hold

onto me, as the words spill everywhere without diminishing
the quantity I still contain; I am a spur, a song,
driven by repetition to say something entirely
new and listening to infants to learn myself.   Take me
up. Uncover me, my hearing
creatures. Feel the funny lump
hardening in my throat as it melts, the weather changes.
In that action of calling hope out
think that you are upon a rock; and now
throw me again.

PATRICIA DEBNEY
Threshold

Today, you are standing at a gate — a wooden gate, the kind you always seem to dream about.

There may be a fence stretching out either side. It may be shadowy, or may not. It may be something you actually run into, by accident or on purpose.

For sure your body has led you here, with its natural piece by piece push and pull, its setting upon the way you and those you love will take.

Meanwhile the edges of things — these solids — grow immaterial. The x or y of them. Their gravity, their mass, direction of travel.

You're at this place. When does one life stop, another begin? The path, the fence, the gate. This blast wave, this hot wind.

ANDREA HOLLAND
Statement

How do you measure the prayers of those living
without God? I have receipts and shall receive:
the petty incantations of the shopkeeper, the late night cigarette,
as censer incense at Tesco petrol station, a taxi purring to your curb,
somebody's cry, tomorrow's forecast — a mix of overcast, sun and about
18 degrees — the filaments of bulb which vibrate as if entranced,
taken up by a holy ghost of sorts.

And when my statement arrives I read the names
like liturgy, all expenditure and cost, and the recitation begins:
Pace Norwich south, child tax credits, National Express, rail cards online,
the East of England Co-op, debits and orders, all the names and numbers
I mouth aloud as *Nunc Dimittis,* in a slow feed through the shredder,
a ticker tape parade of all the journeys and hard days
and not so hard days, 2012–13.

SOPHIE COLLINS
Ed

Ed could see other people's headaches rising like heat haze
Grading papers she thought, 'An era cannot be *self-styled*'
Someone crunched up the gravel of her mind
glimpsed stone lions there on plinths, &
in plain view
turned back round

*

Cropped gelled hair like a boy's
& an adolescent boy's pitch-dark nostrils
late afternoons Ed sets aside marking
attends to her speculative novel-in-progress*

*

November, &
a PDF on translation & globalisation
finally relieved of its duty

------

* *On Gravity* —

… Her mother had died seven years ago. Anna had been sixty-two. She had never known her father, never had a step.

Anna's husband was her father. He frowned when she tripped over things, which happened increasingly frequently. Their marriage had taken place three weeks before Anna's twenty-third birthday.

Today Anna had tripped over the floor divider between kitchen and living room. She had moved herself onto the nearest sofa, gripping her foot in silence. Her husband hadn't looked. He had continued reading, but made sure to broadcast his exasperation for the invisible audience of their marriage with a grimace. He was seven years older than Anna.

Anna's husband was her brother. They would smack each other on the arms and torso, and playfight when there was a good mood. They mocked each other when one of them lost face, whether out in public or before the invisible audience of their marriage. Sometimes the mocking was taken with good grace, other times not.

[CNTD] Sometimes they loved each other. Sometimes they loved each other very much. Most often they loved each other very much after they had endured a period of mutual animosity so wild that it had culminated in Anna plotting to leave, an activity that, far from signalling the end, had the effect of razing all negative feeling. Anna couldn't know, but her husband must have undergone a similar mental process at such times, because it was after this oblivion had been reached that they would finally commune and understand one another as vital.

The cycle had been disrupted by the tripping and the dropping, however; there was fresh tension, beyond the usual run of things.

A university friend Anna was no longer in touch with had once confided in her when they had been sharing a house in South East London at the end of the last century, telling Anna that she had been subject to the most distressing thing Anna had ever heard firsthand. One of the earliest symptoms of her friend's consequent trauma, as she had related it, was the sensation of having her arms pulled down, towards the ground, as though her wrists had been pitched to the Earth with taut guylines|

LILA MATSUMOTO
Or new

Shaded gold, morning's deliberate sequence
stitched
so the metal shows through

Foregrounds small upright figures
and a glade seaming
with sorrel

The entire design
declared in unabated sophistry

> *Cloth is lighter where the sun baffles its border*
> *The closer together the steps are*
> *the denser or stronger the colour*

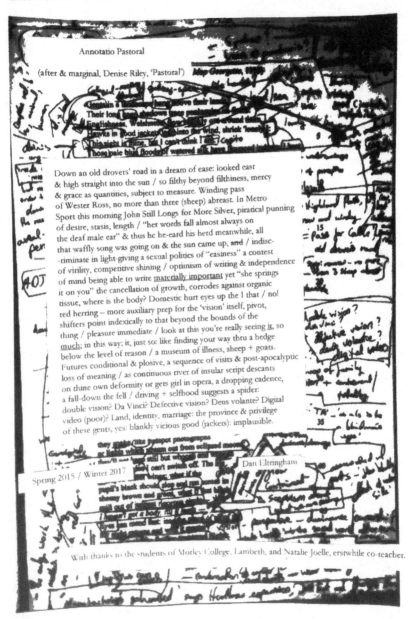

Annotatio Pastoral

(after & marginal, Denise Riley, 'Pastoral')

Down an old drovers' road in a dream of ease: looked east
& high straight into the sun / so filthy beyond filthiness, mercy
& grace as quantities, subject to measure. Winding pass
of Wester Ross, no more than three (sheep) abreast. In Metro
Sport this morning John Still Longs for More Silver, piratical punning
of desire, stasis, length / "her words fall almost always on
the deaf male ear" & thus he he-eard his herd meanwhile, all
that waffly song was going on & the sun came up, and / indisc-
-riminate in light-giving a sexual politics of "easiness" a contest
of virility, competitive shining / optimism of writing & independence
of mind being able to write materially important yet "she springs
it on you" the cancellation of growth, corrodes against organic
tissue, where is the body? Domestic hurt eyes up the 1 that / no!
red herring – more auxiliary prep for the 'vision' itself, pivot,
shifters point indexically to that beyond the bounds of the
thing / pleasure immediate / look at this you're really seeing it, so
much; in this way; it, just so: like finding your way thru a hedge
below the level of reason / a museum of illness, sheep + goats.
Futures conditional & plosive, a sequence of visits & post-apocalyptic
loss of meaning / as continuous river of insular script descants
on thine own deformity or gets girl in opera, a dropping cadence,
a fall-down the fell / driving + selfhood suggests a spider:
double vision? Da Vinci? Defective vision? Deus volante? Digital
video (poor)? Land, identity, marriage: the province & privilege
of these gents, yes: blankly vicious good (jackets): implausible.

Spring 2015 / Winter 2017   Dan Eltringham

With thanks to the students of Morley College, Lambeth, and Natalie Joelle, erstwhile co-teacher.

JEREMY HARDING
My Life as an Infant

A perfect harp lay at my feet
fretting in sleep and singing
I blew on our fingers
like a rainbow or an old tree
to keep off the cold, so perfect
harp sang on and whimpers
to me, think of firelight (he
began) for shadows are
and do, the nights draw in
to your lowest valley, frost folds
out the gingham fields, so ease
into kilter and drink
with me indoors, while your dog
twitches by the stove, sleepy
and flat and quicker than game
the day starts at a sigh from
her blowsy muzzle, morning
doubles to adorn the park you'll
see for yourself a banister of light
through the bare poplars leads
down to the merest flicker
in the grass said perfect harp,
like a rainbow or an old tree
cussing at your shoulder, and
a tune will shortly follow
all your days for lack of nothing
you can put your finger on

LISA ROBERTSON
A Décor

Behind the pool of water
a woman walks slowly; she's
balancing a ceramic
water-urn on her head. On
the table to the far left
a white linen cloth with a
grid of fold-marks is draped

over a dark ornate cloth
with a gilded frieze-like border.
There's a pyramid of figs.
Behind them three windows frame
an azure sky with puffy
clouds, a pillar topped by
a bronze ball, and a linden

tree. Her auburn hair is worn
loose. A seated figure jn
a conventionally pensive
attitude, veiled, occupies
the obscure middle-ground. A
large rectangle of white
fabric is suspended like

an ad-hoc projection screen
between two marble pillars
directly behind the dining
table; a hanging lamp with
three flames throws their shadows
across the wide folds of the
slightly sagging cloth. The floor

is paved in a geometric
pattern with three kinds of marble:
the visible world, known and
inhabited, reveals an eddying.
An indigo woolen wall
covering is edged with
monochrome checkered braid

dyed to match the blue robes
worn in each composition.
On a raised octagonal platform
a threadbare black horsehair
pouf with turned gilt legs
rhymes tidily with the
depicted dining couches.

You can hear the village sleeping.
Carved leaves decorate the
corners of the frames. Come up
overnight an abundance
beneath the linden tree: five
large flat white mushrooms with finely
cut black gills underneath.

ZOË SKOULDING
Summer Fields

After Joan Eardley

as grey pulls back
                    under dry white flicks
the horizon is pure earth
                    levelling with itself

buttermilk stutters over black
                    diagonal lifted under storm-
light this tangled grass
                    pressed into the surface
where daisies explode over
                    go-faster sulphur

pale streaks incline to green
                    while summer runs and
runs in paths colliding
                    as a core of smudged coral
pulses underneath it all

                    glows tangerine
itself a degree of darkness
                    burning into ochre

ÁGNES LEHÓCZKY
Prologos: [Illuminations]

And so when we enter the swimming pool in the middle
of summer, the patient concierge continued guiding us
through semi-lit corridors to the swimming pool, let's
continue to be patient, since today's swim is another
attempt to do it well on the page. To navigate the body
home through language. To home in on the world.
Another attempt to do it wrong again for being in water
has its own paradox. When you are in pool you are not,
in other words. Because the anti-swimmer exists and it
insists on swimming, swimming against the right
direction. The self-doubter who, on behalf of us would
doubt ourselves, the erratic eraser who scraps every
second thought before we could feel, desire, think or
write it down. The anti-scribe in the faithful scribe who
writes a poem to parallel the poem you write. Because
there is always an anti-lover inside the lover inside. A
twin writer resisting writing writing down. An absent
swimmer self always already swimming opposite the
necessary tide contradicting anything we attempt to
understand and so disputing the thing we love. A poem
counterpart inside the poem outside, a parasite poem
gnawing the poem from inside making its way towards
the outside. But my dear parallel scribe, the scribe
inside the patient scribe continued, despite this hooded
figure, this apathetic apparition always appearing at the
edge of the pool, the marginal anti-swimmer, the
phantom counteractor, the drowning instructor, one
must move the body across the horizon as if one's
(eternal) life were at stake ...

ÁGNES LEHÓCZKY'S poetry collections are *Budapest to Babel* (Egg Box, 2008), *Rememberer* (Egg Box, 2012), *Carillonneur* (Shearsman, 2014), *Pool Epitaphs and Other Love Letters* (pamphlet, Boiler House, 2017) and *Swimming Pool* (Shearsman, 2017). She is Lecturer in Creative Writing at the University of Sheffield where she is co-director of the Centre for Poetry and Poetics. The poem in here is from a sequence published in *Swimming Pool* — a book while in the making inspired by a series of correspondences with Denise Riley — for which Denise so generously offered her epigraph 'Time How Short'. [p.155]

ZOË SKOULDING'S recent publications are *Teint: For the Bièvre* (Hafan Books, 2016), *The Museum of Disappearing Sounds* (Seren, 2013) and *Contemporary Women's Poetry and Urban Space: Experimental Cities* (Palgrave Macmillan, 2013). She is Reader in Creative Writing at Bangor University. 'Summer Fields' is a painting by Joan Eardley featured in her 2017 exhibition in Edinburgh, *A Sense of Place*, which Denise Riley recommended. [p.154]

FELICITY ALLEN is an artist and writer. Recent publications include the film *As If They Existed* (with Tom Dale, Turner Contemporary, 2015); a two-volume artists book *Begin Again nos 1–21* (held by Tate and the Getty, 2014) and chapbook *Begin Again Chronicles* (Verisimilitude, 2014). Current projects include a new series of Dialogic Portraits with Refugee Tales. In 1978 she co-founded the Women Artists Slide Library, now archived at Goldsmiths as the Women's Art Library. 'Colouring in' is excerpted from *Begin Again nos 1–21*, a two volume artists book produced from a five year Dialogic Portraits project with 76 sitters. [p.112]

TIM ATKINS' latest book is *On Fathers < On Daughtyrs* (Boiler House Press). The poem in this book is from *The Penguin Book of Japanese Version.* [p.56]

TIFFANY ATKINSON is a Professor of Creative Writing (Poetry) at UEA. Her third collection, *So Many Moving Parts* (Bloodaxe, 2014) was a Poetry Book Society Recommendation and winner of the Roland Matthias Poetry Prize. Her fourth collection, *Dolorimeter*, explores poetry and embarrassment, and frictions between medicine and the arts. [p.91]

EMILY BERRY is the author of *Dear Boy* (Faber & Faber, 2013) and *Stranger, Baby* (Faber & Faber, 2017). A selection of her work appears in *If I'm Scared We Can't Win: Penguin Modern Poets 1*. She is the editor of *The Poetry Review.* [p.135]

RACHEL BLAU DUPLESSIS is a poet, scholar and collagist, known best for feminist and gender related critical work on modern poetry and poetics, for her long poem *Drafts*, and for work on the Objectivist poets. She coedited *The Feminist Memoir Project* with Ann Snitow and she has published a well-regarded feminist trilogy of essays on gender and poetry: *The Pink Guitar*, *Blue Studios*, and *Purple Passages*. Current books of poetry are *Graphic Novella* (collage poems) and *Days and Works* (Hesiodic meditations with newspaper clippings). Poems offered for this anthology are from: *Graphic Novella*, West Lima, Wisconsin: Xexoxial Editions, 2015. All rights reserved. [p.126]

BEN BOREK was born in London in 1980. He has an MA in Creative Writing at UEA (2004). A new verse novel is coming soon from Boiler House Press. He lives in Warsaw. [p.100]

ANDREA BRADY'S books of poetry include *The Strong Room* (Crater, 2016), *Dompteuse* (Bookthug, 2014), *Cut from the Rushes* (Reality Street, 2013), *Mutability: scripts for infancy* (Seagull, 2012), *Wildfire: A Verse Essay on Obscurity and Illumination* (Krupskaya, 2010) and *Vacation of a Lifetime* (Salt, 2001). She is Professor of Poetry at Queen Mary University of London, where she runs the Centre for Poetry and the Archive of the Now. She is also co-publisher of Barque Press. Her article 'Echo, Irony and Repetition in the Writings of Denise Riley' can be found in *Contemporary Women's Writing* 7.2 (2013): 138–156, and 'The Principles of Song: On Denise Riley' in *Toward. Some. Air.,* ed. Fred Wah and Amy De'Ath (Banff: Banff Centre Press, 2015), 13–23. [p.143]

SAM BUCHAN-WATTS is co-editor of clinic press. His pamphlet was published in 2016 in the Faber New Poets series, and he won an Eric Gregory Award the same year. [p.95]

STEPHANIE BURT is Professor of English at Harvard and the author of several books of poetry and literary criticism, most recently *Advice from the Lights* (poems; Graywolf, 2017). Notes: 'Razor Clams' was previously published in the New Zealand magazine *Aotearotica*. [p.86]

JENNA BUTLER is a professor, editor, beekeeper, and market gardener. The author of five award-winning books of poetry and essays, she divides her time between the lecture hall and the off-grid organic farm she runs with her husband in Canada's north country. [p.110]

KIMBERLY CAMPANELLO'S poetry books include *Imagines* (New Dublin Press), *Strange Country* (The Dreadful Press), *Consent* (Doire Press) *and Hymn to Kālī* (Eyewear Publishing). *MOTHERBABYHOME* is forthcoming from zimZalla Avant Objects. A selection from *MOTHERBABYHOME* appeared in September 2017 in Laudanum Publishing's *Chapbook Anthology Volume Two* alongside work by Frances Lock and Abigail Parry. She is a Lecturer in Creative Writing at York St John University. [p.134]

VAHNI CAPILDEO'S tenth publication will be *Venus as a Bear* (Carcanet, 2018), following *Seas and Trees* (Canberra: IPSI, 2017) and *Measures of Expatriation* (Carcanet, 2016) (Forward Prize: Best Collection). Current collaborations include a word/art project with Katy Hastie (Glasgow). She is the Douglas Caster Cultural Fellow at the University of Leeds. [p.106]

IMOGEN CASSELS is from Sheffield and studies in Cambridge. Her poetry has featured or is forthcoming in the *London Review of Books*, *Blackbox Manifold*, *No Prizes*, *Datableed*, *Ambit*, and the London Underground. [p.74]

JOHN CLEGG'S last collection was *Holy Toledo!* (Carcanet, 2016). He works in London as a bookseller. [p.116]

SOPHIE COLLINS grew up in Bergen, North Holland, and now lives in Edinburgh. She is co-editor of *tender*, an online arts quarterly, and editor of *Currently & Emotion* (Test Centre, 2016), an anthology of contemporary poetry translations. *small white monkeys*, a text on self-expression, self-help and shame, was published by Book Works in 2017 as part of a commissioned residency at Glasgow Women's Library. *Who Is Mary Sue?* (Faber & Faber, 2018) is her first poetry collection. [p.147]

KELVIN CORCORAN lives in Brussels. He is the author of 16 books of poetry, including most recently *Facing West,* 2017, and the Medicine Unboxed commissioned *Not Much To Say Really*, 2017. The sequence 'Helen Mania' was a Poetry Book Society choice and the poem 'At the Hospital Doors' was highly commended by the Forward Prize 2017. His work is the subject of a study edited by Professor Andy Brown, *The Poetry Occurs as Song,* 2013. [p.22]

EMILY CRITCHLEY has poetry collections with Boiler House, Barque, Intercapillary, Corrupt, Holdfire, Torque, Oystercatcher, Dusie, Bad and Arehouse presses and a selected writing: *Love / All That / & OK*

(Penned in the Margins, 2011). She is the editor of *Out of Everywhere 2: Linguistically Innovative Poetry by Women in North America & the UK* (Reality Street, 2016). She is Senior Lecturer in English and Creative Writing at the University of Greenwich, London. [p.67]

JAMES CUMMINS teaches English in East London and occasionally writes poems. His books include *Warbler* (DEFAULT, 2009), *speaking off centre* (livestock editions / dusie, 2009), *FLASH/BANG* (Veer, 2011) and *origin of process* (Wild Honey, 2011). [p.78]

IAN DAVIDSON'S most recent poetry publications are *Gateshead and Back* (Crater, 2017), and *On the Way to Work* (Shearman, 2017). Essays are recently published or forthcoming on Diane di Prima and George and Mary Oppen. He lives in Ireland and works at University College, Dublin. [p.139]

AMY DE'ATH'S most recent poetry publication is *ON MY LOVE FOR gender abolition* (New York: Capricious, 2016). She is Lecturer in Contemporary Literature, Culture and Theory at King's College London. [p.10]

PATRICIA DEBNEY'S third collection, *Baby* (Liquorice Fish Books, 2016) looks at loss and dysfunction in a parental relationship; her next is a chapbook of erasures from Tennyson's *In Memoriam*. A former Canterbury Laureate, Patricia is Reader in Creative Writing at the University of Kent. [p.145]

JOE DUNTHORNE was born and brought up in Swansea. His poems have been published in the London Review of Books, Poetry Review and the New Statesman. A collection of his poems is forthcoming from Faber & Faber in summer 2019. He lives in London. The poem in this book was inspired by Denise Riley's 'Poem Beginning with a Line from Proverbs'. [p.44]

KEN EDWARDS' books include *No Public Language: Selected Poems 1975–95* (2006), *Down With Beauty* (2013), *Country Life* (2015) and *a book with no name* (2016). He has been editor/publisher of Reality Street since

1993. He lives in Hastings, where he co-founded the bands Afrit Nebula and The Moors with Elaine Edwards. [p.24]

DANIEL ELTRINGHAM teaches at the University of Sheffield. His first collection, *Cairn Almanac*, was published by Hesterglock Press in 2017. He co-edits Girasol Press and co-runs Electric Arc Furnace, a poetry readings series in Sheffield. [p.150]

American expatriate CARRIE ETTER is Reader in Creative Writing at Bath Spa University and has published three collections, most recently *Imagined Sons* (Seren, 2014). She also edited *Infinite Difference: Other Poetries by UK Women Poets* (Shearsman, 2010) and Linda Lamus's posthumous collection, *A Crater the Size of Calcutta* (Mulfran, 2015). [p.118]

KATY EVANS-BUSH'S poetry collections are *Me and the Dead* and *Egg Printing Explained*, both from Salt, and a pamphlet, *Oscar & Henry*, from Rack Press. *Forgive the Language: Essays on Poetry and Poets* was published by Penned in the Margins in 2015, and most recently her *Broken Cities* was a winner in the 2017 Poetry Business pamphlet competition. She blogs at Baroque in Hackney. [p.60]

ALLEN FISHER is a poet, painter and art historian, lives in Hereford. He has had many shows from Tate Britain to King's Gallery, York to Hereford Museum and over 150 single-author publications to his name. Recently: theoretical work, *Imperfect Fit* and poetry, *Gravity as a consequence of shape*. [p.9]

PETER GIZZI is the author of seven collections of poetry, most recently, *Archeophonics* (finalist for the 2016 National Book Award), *In Defense of Nothing: Selected Poems 1987–2011*, and *Threshold Songs*. [p.3]

JOHN HALL has been reading Denise Riley since 1977. He is the author of 14 collections of poetry, including two complementary Selecteds, and of two volumes of essays on poetics and performance writing. *As a Said Place* (Shearsman) is his most recent collection of poems. [p.34]

ALAN HALSEY'S *Selected Poems 1988–2016* is published by Shearsman. He edited Bill Griffiths' collected poems 1966–96 in three volumes for Reality Street Editions. He is an affiliated poet at Sheffield University's Centre for Poetry and Poetics. [p.18]

NATHAN HAMILTON is a poet and publisher. He is co-founder and managing director of UEA Publishing Project Ltd. and the editor of two anthologies *Dear World & Everyone In It* (Bloodaxe, 2013) and *The Caught Habits of Language* (Donut Press, 2018). [p.89]

JEREMY HARDING is a contributing editor at *The London Review of Books*. His poem for Denise includes a line from one of hers, 'An Infant' (*Marxism for Infants*, Street Editions, 1977), and a phrase from *My Life* by Lyn Hejinian (Burning Deck, 1980). [p.151]

EDMUND HARDY has written a book of experimental philology, *Complex Crosses* (Contraband Books, 2013), and he co-edits Capsule Editions and the magazine of poetry and poetics *Intercapillary Space*. His essays, poems and articles are published in numerous places. The most recent, 'Race, Philology, Capitalism: Nisha Ramayya, Nat Raha, and Daljit Nagra's *Ramayana*' in the Journal of British and Irish Poetry is forthcoming in 2018. The poem in this book incorporates lines from Vince Clarke's 'Only You' performed by Alison Moyet, Denise Riley, Ovid via Arthur Golding, Grimes, Janelle Monáe, Taylor Swift. [p.111]

OZ HARDWICK is a York-based poet, who has been published widely in the UK, Europe and US. His sixth poetry collection, *The House of Ghosts and Mirrors*, was published by Valley Press in September 2017. Oz is Professor of English and Programme Leader for Creative Writing at Leeds Trinity University. [p.33]

MICHAEL HASLAM was born in 1947 and has lived near Hebden Bridge since 1970. 21st Century publications include three books from Arc, a collection of earlier material from Shearsman, and pamphlets from Oystercatcher and from Calder Valley Poetry. [p.28]

SARAH HAYDEN is author of the books *Curious Disciplines: Mina Loy and Avant-Garde Artisthood and Peter Roehr — Field Pulsations* (with Paul Hegarty) and of the chapbooks *Exteroceptive* (Wild Honey), *System Without Issue* (Oystercatcher) and *Turnpikes* (Saḍ Press) with *sitevisit* due in 2018 from Materials. She is a Lecturer in English at the University of Southampton. [p.131]

RALPH HAWKINS has produced a variety of poetry over a number of years as well as co-editing poetry magazines. His latest book is *It Looks Like an Island But Sails Away*, 2015 from Shearsman Books. [p.41]

LYN HEJINIAN is a poet, essayist, teacher, and translator. Her academic work is addressed principally to modernist, postmodern, and contemporary poetry and poetics, with a particular interest in avant-garde movements and the social practices they entail. Her most recent book is *The Unfollowing* (Omnidawn Books, 2016). Belladonna will bring out her prose work, *Positions of the Sun*, in spring 2018. She teaches at the University of California, Berkeley, and is part of the UC Berkeley Humanities Activism coalition, formed immediately after November 8, 2016. [p.72]

COLIN HERD is Lecturer in Creative Writing at the University of Glasgow. His most recent book of poems is *Click & Collect* (Boiler House Press, 2017). He edits www.adjacentpineapple.com [p.120]

DAVID HERD'S collections of poetry include *All Just* (Carcanet, 2012), *Outwith* (Bookthug 2012) and *Through* (Carcanet, 2016). He is Professor of Modern Literature at the University of Kent and a co-organiser of the project Refugee Tales (www.refugeetales.org). [p.123]

SARAH HESKETH holds an MA in creative writing from UEA. Her first full collection of poetry, *Napoleon's Travelling Bookshelf* (Penned in the Margins), was highly commended in the Forward Prize 2010. In 2013 she was poet-in-residence with Age Concern, working with elderly people with dementia, and in 2014 she published *The Hard Word Box* (Penned in the Margins), a collection of poems and interviews inspired by this experience. She currently works for Modern Poetry in

Translation magazine and is working on a Phd on making poetry from oral history. [p.130]

JEFF HILSON has written four books of poetry: *stretchers* (Reality Street, 2006), *Bird bird* (Landfill, 2009), *In The Assarts* (Veer, 2010) and *Latanoprost Variations* (Boiler House Press, 2017). A fifth book, *Organ Music*, is due out from Crater Press in 2018. He also edited *The Reality Street Book of Sonnets* (Reality Street, 2008). He runs Xing the Line poetry reading series in London, and is Reader in Creative Writing at the University of Roehampton. [p.125]

ANDREA HOLLAND is a Lecturer in Creative Writing at UEA. Her collection of poems, *Broadcasting* (Gatehouse Press, 2013) was the winner of the 2012 Norfolk Commission for Poetry. Her first collection, *Borrowed,* was published by Smith/Doorstop in 2007. She has poems in Mslexia, The Rialto, The North and other print/online journals and has collaborated with visual artists on commissioned projects. [p.146]

ALEX HOUEN is author of the poetry chapbook *Rouge States* (Oystercatcher, 2014), and co-author (with Geoff Gilbert) of another chapbook, *Hold! West* (Eyewear, 2016). His debut full collection is titled *Ring Cycle* (Eyewear, 2018). He is co-editor of the online poetry magazine *Blackbox Manifold* and teaches modern literature in the Faculty of English, University of Cambridge. [p.57]

FANNY HOWE has written many books of poetry and fiction. Her most recent collection of poetry is *Second Childhood* from Graywolf Press. She was a Finalist for the National Book Award in 2014 for that book and for the Man Booker International Award, 2015, for her fiction. Her newest collection of prose, *The Needle's Eye,* was published in November 2016. She taught for 45 years and now lives in Massachusetts. [p.5]

PETER HUGHES is a poet and translator. He also runs Oystercatcher Press and is currently based in Cambridge. [p.69]

AMAAN HYDER'S first collection of poetry is *At Hajj* (Penned in the Margins, 2017). His work has appeared in various publications including *The Guardian* and *Poetry Review*. He is a graduate of University College London and the University of East Anglia. [p.70]

JOHN JAMES' *Collected Poems* appeared from Salt in 2002. His more recent works include *Cloud Breaking Sun*, Old Hunstanton: Oystercatcher Press 2012; *Songs in Midwinter for Franco*, Cambridge: Equipage 2014; *Sabots*, Hunstanton: Oystercatcher Press 2015; and, with Bruce McLean, *On Reading J.H. Prynne's Sub Songs*, Ashburton: QoD Press 2016. [p.36]

LINDA KEMP'S poetry publications include *Lease Prise Redux* (Materials, 2016), *Blueprint* (2015), *Immunological* (2014), and an album, *speaking towards* (2015). They edit Enjoy Your Homes Press and co-run Electric Arc Furnace, a poetry reading series in Sheffield. [p.109]

MICHAEL KINDELLAN is a Vice Chancellor's Fellow at the University of Sheffield. Some of his poems are collected in *Not love* (Barque, 2009). [p.140]

CALEB KLACES is the author of the collection *Bottled Air* (Eyewear, 2013) and two pamphlets, *Modern Version* (If a leaf falls, 2017) and *All Safe All Well* (Flarestack, 2011). He is a lecturer at York St John University. [p.92]

RAJIV KRISHNAN did his PhD at Cambridge (1992), and now teaches poetry at the Department of English Literature at the English and Foreign Languages University, Hyderabad. [p.141]

ÁGNES LEHÓCZKY, see NOTES ON EDITORS

TONY LOPEZ is best known for his book *False Memory* (The Figures, 1996; Shearsman, 2012). His most recent collection is *Only More So* (UNO Press, 2011; Shearsman, 2012) the latest of 25 books of poetry, criticism and fiction. He has received awards from the Wingate Foundation, the Society of Authors, the Arts and Humanities Research Council and

Arts Council England. His poetry is featured in *The Art of the Sonnet* (Harvard), *The New Concrete* (Hayward), *Twentieth-Century British and Irish Poetry* (Oxford), *The Dark Would* (Apple Pie), *Vanishing Points* (Salt), *The Reality Street Book of Sonnets*, *Other: British and Irish Poetry since 1970* (Wesleyan), and *Conductors of Chaos* (Picador). His critical writings are collected in *Meaning Performance: Essays on Poetry* (Salt, 2006) and *The Poetry of W.S. Graham* (Edinburgh University Press, 1989). He edited *The Text Festivals: Language Art and Material Poetry* (University of Plymouth Press, 2013) and co-edited *Poetry & Public Language* (Shearsman, 2007) with Anthony Caleshu. He taught for many years at Plymouth University and was appointed the first Professor of Poetry there in 2000 and Emeritus Professor in 2009. [p.105]

KYLE LOVELL is based in Canterbury. His work has been published in *Magma* and *The Kindling*, and he is the editor at Fathomsun Press. [p.80]

TOM LOWENSTEIN was born in 1941 and read English at Cambridge. He taught in London comprehensive schools 1966–71, then at Northwestern University, Evanston, Ill. 1971–74. From 1975 to the present, did ethnographic fieldwork in northwest Alaska. He lives with family and continues to work in London. His books include *Filibustering in Samsara* (Many Press, 1987); *The Things that were Said of Them* (University of California Press, 1990); *Ancient Land: Sacred Whale* (Bloomsbury and Farrar, Strauss & Giroux, 1993); *Ancestors and Species* (Shearsman, 2005); *Ultimate Americans* (University of Alaska Press, 2008); *Conversation of Murasaki* (Shearsman, 2009); *From Culbone Wood — in Xanadu* (Shearsman, 2013); *After the Snowbird, Comes the Whale* — serialized in *Fortnightly Review*, 2018. [p.50]

LILA MATSUMOTO'S publications include *Allegories from my Kitchen* (Sad Press) and *Soft Troika* (If a Leaf Falls Press). *Urn and Drum*, her first full poetry collection, came out with Shearsman in 2018. Lila co-edits the poetry and arts magazine *FRONT HORSE* and teaches creative writing at the University of Nottingham. [p.149]

SO MAYER writes feminisms between poetry and film criticism. Her most recent books are *(O)* (Arc, 2015), *kaolin, or How Does a Girl Like You Get to Be a Girl Like You* (Lark, 2015), *Political Animals: The New Feminist Cinema* (IB Tauris, 2015) and *From Rape to Resistance: Taking Back the Screen* (self-published ebook, 2017). [p.75]

GERALDINE MONK has been an incurable poet since the 1970s. Her *Selected Poems* was published in 2003 by Salt Publishing. Her latest book *They Who Saw The Deep* was published in the USA by Parlor Press/ Free Verse Editions in April 2016. She is an affiliated poet at the Centre for Poetry and Poetics, University of Sheffield. [p.19]

ROD MENGHAM is Reader in Modern English Literature at Cambridge, Curator of Works of Art at Jesus College and publisher of Equipage poetry pamphlets. His writings include: *Unsung: New and Selected Poetry* (2001), *Chance of a Storm* (2015); *Speedometry* [translations of Andrzej Sosnowski poems](2014); and with Marc Atkins *Moving Still* (2014). [p.54]

MARIANNE MORRIS was born in Toronto in 1981, and raised in London, UK. Her most recent collection, *Word/World*, came out with Boiler House Press in the UK (2017). She has her BA and MPhil from Cambridge University, and was awarded the Harper-Wood travel and writing scholarship from St John's College, Cambridge, in 2008. She received her doctorate in contemporary poetry from University College Falmouth in 2013. Morris' first poetry book was published by Enitharmon Press in the UK in 2013, and one of the poems in it was selected for the Forward Prize Anthology in 2015. She ran a small chapbook press in the UK for 10 years called Bad Press. [p.136]

WENDY MULFORD lives between Papa Westray, Orkney and Suffolk. She lives with composer Gordon Crosse and Clumber aristocrat and renegade, Winterholt Red Rose, alias Freya. Has a beautiful thatched 17c cottage to sell. Apply Wendy. The poem in this anthology is published as a Poem Card from Shorehouse, PAPA WESTRAY, Orkney, in an edition of 50. [p.4]

ALICE NOTLEY has published over forty books of poetry, including (most recently) *Benediction*, *Negativity's Kiss*, and *Certain Magical Acts*. She lives in Paris, France. [p.20]

WANDA O'CONNOR is a poet and scholar of contemporary poetry and poetics. Work is available from the chapbook *damascene road passaggio* (above/ground press); *Wretched Strangers* (Boiler House Press, 2018); *Bad Kid Catullus* (Sidekick Books, 2017); *Poetry Wales, Asymptote, and others*. [p.132]

SIMON PERRIL'S poetry publications include *Beneath* (Shearsman, 2015), *Archilochus on the Moon* (Shearsman 2013), *Newton's Splinter* (Open House 2012), *Nitrate* (Salt 2010), *A Clutch of Odes* (Oystercatcher, 2009), and *Hearing is Itself Suddenly a Kind of Singing* (Salt, 2004). As a critic he has written widely on contemporary poetry, including editing the books *The Salt Companion to John James*, and *Tending the Vortex: The Works of Brian Catling*. He is Reader in Contemporary Poetic Practice at De Montfort University, Leicester. [p.63]

ADAM PIETTE co-edits the poetry journal *Blackbox Manifold* with Alex Houen, is author of *Remembering and the Sound of Words, Imagination at War*, and *The Literary Cold War*, and is Professor of Modern Literature at the University of Sheffield. [p.81]

FRANCES PRESLEY'S publications include *Paravane* (Salt, 2004); *Myne* (Shearsman, 2006); *Lines of Sight* (Shearsman, 2009); *An Alphabet for Alina* with Peterjon Skelt (Five Seasons, 2012); *Halse for Hazel* (Shearsman, 2014) which received an Arts Council award, and *Sallow* (Leafe, 2016). Her work is in the anthologies *Infinite Difference* (2010), *Ground Aslant: radical landscape poetry* (2011) and *Out of Everywhere2* (2015). I have long admired Denise Riley's work and saw her often in London in the 1980s and '90s. I recently wrote about her in 'Experimental poetry and feminism? London 1980–86' (*Clasp: late modernist poetry in London in the 1970s*, ed. Robert Hampson and Ken Edwards, 2016), and I also responded at the time in 'The grace of being common: the search for the implicit subject in the work of Denise Riley', *Southfields* 5(2) and *How2*, 1999. [p.6]

MEGHAN PURVIS has an M.A. and Ph.D. from the University of East Anglia, as well as an M.F.A. from North Carolina State University. Her translation of Beowulf was published by Penned in the Margins and won the 2011 Stephen Spender Prize for literary translation. She is working on her first novel. [p.47]

DERYN REES-JONES' *What It's Like to be Alive: Selected Poems* was published by Seren in 2016. She is Professor of Poetry at the University of Liverpool. [p.121]

PETER RILEY was born in Stockport in 1940 and recently retired to Hebden Bridge after living for 28 years in Cambridge. He is the author of fifteen books of poetry, most recently *Due North* (Shearsman 2015) which was shortlisted for the Forward Best Collection Prize, and two pamphlets issued by Calder Valley Poetry, *Pennine Tales* 2016 and *Hushings* 2017. [p.39]

Over the years LISA ROBERTSON has been very grateful to wear some very beautiful garments given to her by Denise Riley: A harlequin-like summer coat from Sweden, an English wool and linen translucent tunic, a silk scarf with a William Morris wallpaper pattern, faceted jade beads. They have seemed co-extensive with the poems. [p.152]

PETER ROBINSON'S most recent publications are the novel, *September in the Rain* (2016), and *Collected Poems 1976–2016* (2017). *The Sound Sense of Poetry*, which includes chapters touching on themes in Denise Riley's work, is published by Cambridge University Press in 2018. Professor of English and American Literature at the University of Reading, he is also poetry editor for Two Rivers Press. [p.29]

SOPHIE ROBINSON is a poet. She lives between London and Norwich, where she teaches Creative Writing at the University of East Anglia. She is the author of *A* and *The Institute of Our Love in Disrepair*. Recent work has appeared in *n+1*, *The White Review*, *Poetry Review*, *The Brooklyn Rail* and *Ploughshares*. The title of the poem offered here is taken from Denise Riley's 'wherever you are, be somewhere else'. [p.14]

LISA SAMUELS is the author of sixteen books of poetry, memoir, and prose — mostly poetry. Her recent works include *Symphony for Human Transport* (2017) and *Foreign Native* (2018). She also publishes essays and soundworks as well as editing books, collaborating with composers, and working with film. Since 2006 she has lived in New Zealand, where she earns her living as an academic while also raising her son. [p.45]

ANNA SELBY is a poet and naturalist. Her poems often explore our relationship with water and are studies of different species, written en plein air, that share a sense of compassion and attentiveness to the environment. Her poem for Denise is an outcry. Her willing herself to be braver. [p.97]

ZOË SKOULDING, see NOTES ON EDITORS

SIMON SMITH is a poet, translator and essayist. His latest book, *Day In, Day Out* (Parlor Press, 2017) was published in the U.S.A., and his selected poems appeared in 2016 from Shearsman Books, *More Flowers Than You Could Possibly Carry*. The poem included here comes from a sequence, 'Municipal Love Poems'. [p.15]

SAMUEL SOLOMON is author of *Special Subcommittee* (Commune Editions, 2017) and translator, with Jennifer Kronovet and Faith Jones, of *The Acrobat: Selected Poems of Celia Dropkin* (Tebot Bach, 2014). He teaches in the School of English at the University of Sussex where he is Co-Director of the Centre for the Study of Sexual Dissidence. His writings on the work of Denise Riley can be found in the *Journal of British and Irish Innovative Poetry* and his forthcoming book *Lyric Pedagogy and Marxist Feminism: Social Reproduction and the Institutions of Poetry* (Bloomsbury, 2018). [p.103]

ANDREW SPRAGG was born and lives in London. He has written for *Hix Eros*, *The Quietus* and *PN Review*. Recent books include *Now Too How Soon* (Contraband Books, 2017), *OBJECTS* (Red Ceiling Press, 2014), *A Treatise on Disaster* (Contraband Books, 2013) and *To Blart & Kid* (Like This Press, 2013). [p.48]

GEORGE SZIRTES was born in Hungary in 1948; he published his first book of poems, *The Slant Door*, in 1979 which won the Faber Prize. He has published many since then, *Reel* (2004) winning the T S Eliot Prize, for which he has been twice shortlisted since. His latest book is *Mapping the Delta* (Bloodaxe, 2016). [p.13]

REBECCA TAMÁS is a London based poet, who recently completed a PhD in Creative and Critical Writing at UEA, under the supervision of Denise Riley. Rebecca's pamphlet *Savage*, was published by Clinic Press this year, and she has most recently had work in *The London Review of Books*, *Poetry Review*, *Minerva Platform* and *The White Review*. Rebecca was joint winner of the 2016 Manchester Poetry Prize, and is the Fenton Emerging Writer 2017. [p.43]

HARRIET TARLO is a poet and academic with an interest in gender, landscape, place and environment. Her publications include *Field*; *Poems 2004-2014*; *Poems 1990-2003* (Shearsman 2016, 2014, 2004); *Nab* (etruscan 2005) and, with Judith Tucker, *Sound Unseen* and *behind land* (Wild Pansy, 2013 and 2015). She is editor of *The Ground Aslant: An Anthology of Radical Landscape Poetry* (Shearsman, 2011) and special poetry editor for *Plumwood Mountain* 4:2 (2017). Her critical work appears in volumes by Salt, Palgrave, Rodopi and Bloodaxe and in *Pilot*, *Jacket*, *English* and the *Journal of Ecocriticism*. Her collaborative work with Tucker has shown at galleries including the Catherine Nash Gallery Minneapolis, 2012; Musee de Moulages, Lyon, 2013; Southampton City Art Gallery 2013-14; The Muriel Barker Gallery, Grimsby and the New Hall College Art Collection, Cambridge, 2015. She is a Reader in Creative Writing at Sheffield Hallam University. Notes on 'Two Cut Flowers for Denise Riley': (i) references Alina Szapocznjkow and Helena Włodarczyk; (ii) references Rothko. [p.119]

MARTIN THOM works as a translator, editor and historian; his *Republics, Nations and Tribes* was published by Verso in 1995. A long poem entitled *Fair* is to appear as a pamphlet with *infernal methods* in 2018. Notes on the poem: Ovid, *Metamorphoses*, Bk. VIII, ll. 738–877; D'Arcy Wentworth Thompson, *On Growth and Form* [1917]. [p.98]

SCOTT THURSTON is a poet, mover/dancer and educator living in Manchester, UK. He has published twelve books and chapbooks of poetry including three full-length collections with Shearsman Books. He co-edits the *Journal of British and Irish Innovative Poetry*, and co-organises The Other Room poetry reading series. The epigraph to his sonnet for Denise is a sentence from her book *Time Lived, Without Its Flow*, whilst the quotation inside the poem is dialogue from Chris Marker's film *San Soleil*. [p.32]

NICK TOTTON is a body psychotherapist, trainer, supervisor and writer currently based in Cornwall. He has known Denise for about forty years. He recently started writing poetry again after a twenty-year hiatus, and has just published *Cold Calling* (Equipage). [p.26]

JUHA VIRTANEN'S publications include *Back Channel Apraxia*, *-LAND*, and *Poetry and Performance During the British Poetry Revival 1960–1980: Event and Effect*, which features a chapter on Denise Riley and a transcript of an interview with her. He co-edits DATABLEED together with Eleanor Perry, and works at the University of Kent. [p.79]

KEITH WALDROP is the author of *Selected Poems* (Omnidawn), *Transcendental Studies* (University of California Press, National Book Award 2009), and more than a dozen other books of poems. He has also published a novel, *Light While There Is Light* (Dalkey Archive), a book of collages, *Several Gravities* (Siglio,) and translated Baudelaire's *Flowers of Evil* and *Poems in Prose* as well as contemporary French authors Anne-Marie Albiach, Claude Royet-Journoud, Paol Keineg, Jean Grosjean etc. He is retired from teaching at Brown University and lives in Providence, RI. Notes: 'Theme' appeared in *The Locality Principle* (Avec Books, 1995). [p.66]

ROSMARIE WALDROP'S recent books are *Gap Gardening: Selected Poems*, *Driven to Abstraction*, *Curves to the Apple* (all New Directions), and *White is a Color* (Guillemot Press). Her collected essays, *Dissonance (if you are interested)* were published by University of Alabama Press, two novels, *The Hanky of Pippin's Daughter* and *A Form/ of Taking/ It All,* by Northwestern University Press. She has translated 14 volumes of Edmond Jabès's work (her memoir, *Lavish Absence: Recalling and Rereading Edmond Jabès,* is out from Wesleyan UP) as well as books by Emmanuel Hocquard, Jacques Roubaud, and, from the German, Friederike Mayröcker, Elke Erb, Oskar Pastior, Gerhard Rühm, Ulf Stolterfoht. [p.65]

GEOFF WARD has been publishing poetry since the 1970s, most recently in *Worry Dream* (Equipage, Cambridge: 2013). He wrote the first book on the New York School of Poets, *Statutes of Liberty*, (1993: 2001) first published by Macmillan in the Language, Discourse & Society series co-edited by Denise Riley, as was *Poets on Writing: Britain 1970 to 1991* to which he contributed an essay, 'Objects that Come Alive at Night'. His first novel *You're Not Dead* was published in New York in 2016. An editor of *The Cambridge Quarterly*, he has also written and presented programmes on American literature for BBC Radio 3. Currently Principal of Homerton College, he is also Deputy Vice-Chancellor of the University of Cambridge, Acting Director of the Fitzwilliam Museum, and an Honorary Fellow of Harris Manchester College, Oxford. [p.83]

RACHEL WARRINER is a poet and art historian based in London. She has published the poetry books *Primary* (DEFAULT), *Detritus* (DEFAULT/Dusie Press), *Eleven Days* (Runamok Press) and *Fine Lament* (Critical Documents). Her scholarly texts have been published in journals such as *Artefact*, *Courtauld Books Online,* and *The Irish University Review* and her book *Pain and Politics in Postwar Feminist Art: Activism in the work of Nancy Spero* is forthcoming from IB Tauris. [p.102]

CAROL WATTS is Professor of Literature and Poetics at the University of Sussex. Her most recent work includes *Dockfield* (Equipage, 2017), and the collection *When Blue Light Falls* (Shearsman, 2018). [p.37]

JOHN WELCH'S *Collected Poems* appeared from Shearsman in 2008, at the same time as 'Dreaming Arrival', an account of his personal experience of psychoanalysis. In 1975 he founded The Many Press which he ran for the next 25 years publishing books and pamphlets of new poetry. [p.96]

J.T. WELSCH has published six chapbooks, including *Orchids* (Salt, 2010), *The Ruin* (Annexe, 2015), and *Hell Creek Anthology* (Sidekick, 2015). His recent criticism includes essays on John Berryman, Elizabeth Bishop, and Gertrude Stein. He lives in York, where he lectures at the University of York. [p.115]

NIGEL WHEALE'S books include *Writing and Society. Literacy, Print and Politics, 1590–1660* (Routledge 1999) and *Raw Skies. New and Selected Poems* (Shearsman, 2005). He lived and worked in Orkney from 2003 to 2016. [p.59]

The World Speaking Back
... to Denise Riley

A CIP record for this book is available from the British Library.

Design and typesetting by Emily Benton.
emilybentonbookdesigner.co.uk
Typeset in Arnhem
Printed and bound in the UK by Imprint Digital.

Distributed by
NBN International,
10 Thornbury Road
Plymouth PL6 7PP
t. +44 (0)1752 2023102
e. cservs@nbninternational.com

ISBN 978-1-911343-39-4